Nathan
Cartwright's

WEEK TO REMEMBER

Phillip G.D. Jones

Disclaimer

This book is a work of fiction. Names, characters, places, events, and incidents are either the products of the author's imagination or used in a fictitious manner. The author has crafted this story for entertainment purposes and does not intend to depict real-world events or individuals.

Dedication

To my wonderful wife, Lizzie: your love, support, and encouragement have been my greatest inspiration. Without you, this book would have remained just a dream.

About the Author

Gavin Douglas was born in 1962. After completing an apprenticeship in toolmaking and working primarily in the injection molding industry, he joined the Royal Air Force in 1986.

Throughout a remarkable 32-year career, Gavin retired as a senior commissioned officer. He continues to work within the military domain, representing an international agency.

This novel is Gavin's first—and possibly only—venture into writing, depending on its reception. His bucket list inspired it, and it was a personal challenge to explore new horizons.

Interestingly, Phillip Jones is Gavin's birth name, which he discovered at the age of 48 when he met his birth mother for the first time. This reunion also introduced him to a loving extended family. Despite this revelation, Gavin cherishes the fond memories of his late adoptive parents, who shaped the man he is today. That, however, is a story for another time!

Gavin is married to his wonderful wife, Lizzie, and together they have four grown-up sons. In his spare time, he enjoys rock drumming and motorcycle trail riding—perhaps writing will join the list in the future.

Table Of Contents

Chapter 1

In your Own Words...

The station's interview room was exactly what I expected— grey walls, a plain wooden desk, and two matching wooden chairs. As I gathered my thoughts, I noticed the desk was bolted to the floor. Strange. Who'd want to steal it? Just dragging it out the door would be impossible. No two-way mirror here either, but that made sense— this was Halifax, not New York City. At least the room was warm.

Julia sat to my left, quiet for the last five minutes. Her silence wasn't comforting; it only made her nervousness more obvious. Her hand shook as she pulled a leather-backed notebook from her briefcase and opened it on the desk. It was brand new—probably bought just for today to make her look more "official." But I could tell she was out of her depth.

Julia wasn't a lawyer. She was my social worker. At 17, I needed a parent or guardian present for this interview, and Julia was the closest thing I had. She'd been assigned to my case two years ago and had overseen my last two foster homes. We had a bond—she made me feel like more than just another case. She genuinely cared.

Julia was also beautiful—mid-twenties, single, and trying hard to look authoritative. She styled her blonde hair in a shoulder-length bob, probably to seem more professional, though it only made her cuter. Even with her curves hidden under a matching jacket and trousers, she couldn't resist four-inch heels or leaving the top too many buttons of her silk blouse undone. I had to admit: Julia always looked

1

stunning.

But now wasn't the time for those thoughts. Two detectives were on their way, and the scent of heavy perfume hit the room before the door even opened. I shifted in my chair, realizing Julia's looks wouldn't be a distraction this time. The door creaked open, and two female detectives entered. The younger one scraped her chair across the floor as she sat down, the sound grating like nails on a chalkboard. I felt the hair on the back of my neck rise. My nerves were stretched thin. The older detective adjusted her round glasses, giving me what I guess was supposed to be a reassuring smile.

"Hello, Nathan," she began. "I'm Jennifer Green, and with me is Lucy Dusnough." The name "Dusnough" sounded a lot like "Does Nowt," which was fitting—she didn't speak, just jotted notes in a cheap notepad that screamed government budget. Jenny Green, the older detective, continued, "Feel free to call me Jenny. And, of course, you know Miss Featherstone." Julia gave my hand a brief, comforting touch before quickly pulling away.

Jenny explained that while this was "just a chat," she needed my permission to record the interview. Julia tensed beside me, ready to object, but I gave a small smile and nodded. Julia's eyes widened, questioning my decision, but then she relaxed, returning my smile nervously. Jenny nodded and pressed the button to start recording. She stated the date, time, and the names of everyone present. Then she leaned forward, studying me for a moment that felt much longer than it probably was.

She looked to be in her mid-thirties—short, curly black hair pulled back into a tiny ponytail that did nothing to flatter her round face. Her tired trouser suit had seen better days, and the streaks of grey at her hairline peeked through a poorly applied foundation. Those imperfections made me feel a little less tense. "How are you feeling,

Nathan?" Jenny asked, her tone casual. With a possible manslaughter charge hanging over me, that was her opening question? She gestured towards the bandage wrapped around my neck and shoulder, clearly referring to my injury.

"It's not too bad, Miss," I replied, emphasizing her title to highlight my youth and vulnerability. "But it does hurt if I move too quickly. At least it's not bleeding anymore, so the nurse must've done a good job patching me up." It was a lie—it didn't hurt at all. The seven stitches were already going slack, though the wound itched like crazy. But the last thing I wanted was to draw attention. I dusted off the crinkly paper suit they'd given me, forcing a small smile. "Only my pride hurts," I added, quickly dropping my eyes to feign shame.

Jenny sighed sympathetically. "I'm sorry about that, Nathan. But I'm sure you understand why we had to remove your clothes. "I nodded, playing along. Then came the question I'd been dreading: "Tell me, in your own words, what happened last night. You were seen leaving The Wellington pub around 9 p.m., alone. "Lucy, or "Does Not," smoothed the page of her notebook and poised her pen, ready to record every word.

Julia and I exchanged a quick glance. Her concern was written all over her face. I'd already told her the whole story—how they found me in an alley off Hudson Street, half-conscious, bleeding from the back of my neck. I was lying on the chest of a dead teenager whose face had been battered beyond recognition. Worse still, I had a stiletto knife in my hand. It wasn't a good look.

Julia gave me the smallest of signals—a flicker of her eyes, a slight curve of her lips—trusting me to go ahead. It was the kind of unspoken understanding that formed between two relative youngsters who knew they were probably out of their depth. However, having already heard my story, I guess she realized I could bullshit with the best.

Resting my elbows on the table, I cradled my forehead in my hands, pretending to wince before slowly sitting back. Play the game, lad. Play the game. With all the confusion of a 17-year-old caught in a nightmare, I looked Jenny Green in the eye and began: "Well, Miss, all I can remember is this…"

Chapter 2

Dirty Deeds Done Dirt Cheap

"Let's not forget that Nathan is the real victim here," Julia began, her voice soft but insistent.

"There are actually two victims we know of, Miss Featherstone," DI Green cut in, sharp as ever. "And if I may suggest, the real victim is David Kelsey—since he's the one who ended up dead."

So that was his name: David Kelsey. Knowing the victim's name is supposed to make them more human and easier to empathize with. But honestly? I'd rather remember him as the cocky chav who fancied himself a "gangster," just because he talked with that fake Jamaican accent a lot of the younger lot seemed to adopt. Seriously, who hires kids like him? Fast-food joints, probably—and fittingly, that's where most of them spend their nights, loitering outside.

"Listen," I interrupted, steering the conversation back. "I've got no problem telling you what I know. Maybe it'll help me make sense of all this, and I've got nothing to hide. So where do you want me to start?"

DI Green leaned in slightly. "Why not start with your night at the Wellington on Green Street? Walk me through it—who was with you?"

That part I remembered clearly. It was the later hours that got hazy. I took a deep breath and began recounting the night as steadily as I could.

"Billy Green met me, same as usual, on the corner of Nelson Street around 8:30 p.m."

Billy always showed up early. I knew why—home wasn't exactly the picture-perfect family you see on TV. His dad was one of those slimy blokes: charming to outsiders, especially women, but treated his wife Mary like shit. Not abusive, but dismissive. Mary, though—she was something else. MILF material, for sure, even though she never wore makeup. Lucky for Billy, he'd inherited her better traits.

"We set off at a brisk pace towards the Wellington," I continued.

Billy, as usual, couldn't decide whether to tuck his shirt into his faded jeans or leave it hanging loose. He fussed over it until the bottom got too creased, making the decision for him. That was Billy— quirky and good-natured in a way that drew people in, especially women.

He wasn't drop-dead handsome, but he had something better—those eyes, that smile. Girls flocked to him, even one's way out of his league. I didn't mind; it took the attention off me. Not that I was looking to impress anyone that night—it was Friday, beer o'clock, and I had no interest in chatting up girls.

"The Wellington was pretty busy for a Friday," I said, remembering the crowd.

"Busy" meant maybe 30 people—pubs like the Wellington didn't thrive on selling pints anymore. Food was where the money was, and that drew in couples and older patrons, not the usual rowdy chav crowd. George, the manager, ran a tight ship. He had a strict rule about kids misbehaving in his pub. Anyone who showed up with children got a firm reminder: "This is a licensed establishment. If your kids don't behave, you'll be asked to leave."

Most folks got the message right away—probably from the noticeable absence of children running around. The atmosphere suited everyone—peaceful, grown-up, and full of patrons who actually spent money. Billy and I were welcome, though. We'd been coming for two years and always stayed out of trouble. Both of us could pass for twenty without much effort.

"Did you recognize anyone there that night?" DI Green asked, her tone probing.

Her partner, "Does Nowt," tilted her head and flicked her long brown hair behind her ear, waiting for my answer.

"Not really," I admitted. "There were a few familiar faces, but I couldn't tell you their names."

"Does Nowt" jotted a quick note on her pad.

"Around 10:30, Billy said he wanted to hit the Majestic." I shrugged. "I wasn't in the mood for clubbing. I was starving and had that annoying throbbing in my head that wouldn't quit. It was too late to grab food at the bar, so I figured I'd head home and eat there."

Billy spent the next five minutes teasing me, calling me a "pussy" and a "fag" with his usual playful grin. After one last friendly punch to my shoulder, he promised to see me on Monday at school.

And that's when things got strange.

I'd planned to head straight home, but as soon as I stepped out of the pub, I turned left instead of right. I zipped up my knockoff NY Giants jacket, feeling the sudden chill that had settled over the night.

The smell from the KFC around the corner hit me hard—oddly intense, almost inviting. For some reason, it didn't smell greasy or off-putting, just... weirdly good.

7

"That's when I saw him," I said, the memory snapping back into focus.

David Kelsey and his bigger, dumber sidekick stood on the corner, both of them in the usual uniform—black hoodies and jeans, hoods pulled up tight. You know the type: trying to look tough, blending into the shadows, but failing miserably.

And this really gets on my nerves. These chavs always refer to themselves as "gangsters" but won't show their faces. Everyone knows who Al Capone and the Kray Twins were—and what they looked like. They sought to be well-known in their communities. Don't get me wrong; you would have been a fool to cross them, but most of their communities respected them. And why not? Many of their ill-gotten gains helped the poorer individuals in those communities. They commanded respect, unlike these little shits.

"Normally, I would have crossed the street and kept a low profile, but it was clear our little gangsters were physically harassing what looked like a young couple in their twenties. I thought the guy would have flattened the two chavs on any other day, but he seemed aware that his girlfriend/fiancée/wife was in a vulnerable position. One slip or mistake could have ended badly for her. It was her fate that changed my intention.

"I opened with, 'Are you all right, mate?' clearly addressing the guy being pushed while approaching the chavs from the blindside. This caught Kelsey's mate's attention; he looked over his shoulder while still gripping the target's shoulder. Unlike Kelsey, wielding a knife that clearly attracted the victim's full attention, the other dickhead appeared unarmed. This made him an easy target, and with a quick lunge to the left, I caught him with a beauty of a right, causing his nose to explode in an eruption of blood.

"Falling to the ground while clutching his bloody and probably broken nose, he attempted to say something menacing, but it sounded funny, like someone trying to sing with a blocked nose. Taking a step closer, he surprisingly jumped to his feet, turned, and ran off down the street, one hand clutching his nose and the other trying to prevent his jeans from falling down and tripping him.

Yeah, very gangster!

"Kelsey focused entirely on me. I thought the gentleman being harassed would have used the opportunity to lay Kelsey out, but impressively, his first thought was to extract his young lady from the scene. Sensibly, he walked her away as quickly as her four-inch stilettos would allow back toward the Wellington without even a thank-you. I didn't mind; I had more pressing matters with young Kelsey.

You can read so much from someone's eyes—the gateway to the soul. When dating, if your potential partner maintains eye contact when you're speaking, your job's done, and you can relax and enjoy each other's company. Kelsey was no different.

"I could almost hear his thought process with a mere glance. He was clearly in panic mode, unsure whether to break free and run or maintain his portrayal as a hard man. Unfortunately for him, he chose the latter and clumsily swung the knife at me.

Firstly, you don't swing a knife. Even to a non-physicist, it takes longer for an object to travel in an arc than in a straight line. Perhaps it was a warning, and he didn't have the guts to finish the job. Either way, it wouldn't influence my approach. The little shit needed to be taught a lesson, and I was going to provide it!

"I'm sorry, but that's all I can remember." I lifted my head and looked at DI Green. I didn't have to feign confusion; it was the truth.

"That's okay." DI Green smiled. "That's what we assumed happened; we just needed to hear it from you. Unless you have anything else to tell us, you're free to go."

"So... I'm not being charged with his murder?" I asked, genuinely surprised while exchanging glances with Julia.

"No, you're fine, Nathan. Although I am curious... You mentioned 'murder' and not 'murders.' Aren't you forgetting Mr. Shaw, Mr. Kelsey's friend?"

"I only busted his nose, and when he ran off, he was certainly alive." I was riddled with curiosity about her direction.

"You're correct, Nathan; he was alive when he left you, suggesting the person who attacked you and Mr. Kelsey then broke Mr. Shaw's neck. We know it couldn't have been you since he was found dumped in an alley half a mile from where you were."

I was about to ask for more details when Julia spoke.

"I'm glad Nathan could help. And don't worry, if you need to speak to us again, we won't be skipping the country. You know where to find us. Please contact me rather than going straight to Nathan."

"Does Nowt?" then threw me by speaking for the first time to ask if they could give me a lift home.

To be fair, I hadn't paid much attention to her; she was very good at being "grey," the type who could walk past you in the street, and you couldn't describe her later. Looking closer, I wondered how she had gone unnoticed. Despite lacking makeup or extreme skill in applying the "minimal look," she was quite attractive. Her shoulder-length, straight brown hair didn't have a distinct style, but it must have been an expensive cut. Her cream blouse and faded denim jeans didn't attract attention, but if you looked closely, they concealed a very toned and athletic body. Overall, a very understated look, except for the shoes. When was the last time you saw a female police officer in

Christian Louboutin's heels? She could have gotten away with it if she hadn't crossed her legs. It's lost on most men, but I knew that high-heeled shoes with red soles were bloody expensive.

"That's very kind of you," Julia responded while rising to her feet. "But I'll drop Nathan off. It's on my way home."

I didn't have much to say, so I didn't. I stood, aware of the itchy stitches—they'd need to come out when I returned home—and followed Julia out of the interview room. DI Green escorted us to the foyer desk.

While being officially booked out, DI Green disappeared briefly, only to return with a transparent bag filled with my clothes.

"It appears we won't need these after all. If you'd like to change in that room, you can leave what you're wearing in the bag, and you're free to go. Thank you for talking to us, and enjoy the rest of your week-end if you can." She offered her hand.

I gave her hand a weak shake and thanked her, not really knowing what I was thanking her for.

Stepping outside the station into the crisp Saturday sunshine, we walked to Julia's little red KIA Soul without speaking. I considered teasing her about her parking since she'd only nearly made it between the lines, but I decided it wasn't worth the trouble. Sometimes, it's not worth breaking a silence that may lead to a conversation you're either unprepared for or want. My reason was the latter.

I had too many questions. Who killed that Shaw dude? And more importantly, how did someone manage to knock me unconscious without me sensing their presence? I didn't give a single shit about Shaw or Kelsey—the world would be a better place without either contaminating it—but I needed to know who else was involved, hope-fully before the police.

I did my best not to slam Julia's door. The comforting scent of her perfume lingered in the upholstery.

"Chin up, Ringo," she said with a smile while fastening her seat belt. "It appears you've just gotten away with murder." She burst into genuine laughter!

I joined in. She was right, of course. I thanked her for her support, and she shrugged while looking over her right shoulder to reverse the car.

"It's my job."

I wasn't sure if she really meant it. I was more concerned with how close she came to clipping the Audi with her left front end. I'd had enough of the police for one day.

Chapter 3

Coffee and Biscuits

J ulia's taste in music was even worse than her parking. If what we were listening to was supposed to be R&B, then I guess I've been living under a rock. To me, it sounded like a bunch of amateurs rehearsing for the first time—half the band missing and the other half wondering where they went. At least she kept the volume low, so it was more background static than anything offensive.

She didn't waste time getting to the point.

"So, any plans for the weekend now that you're a free man?" she asked, glancing at me with a quick, playful flick of her eyes before locking back onto the road.

The way Julia sat told me everything I needed to know about her driving: rigid and upright, gripping the wheel in a textbook 10-and-2, like a student trying to impress her instructor. I could tell that parking had given her away—careful drivers are always the worst at it. And the seat? It was pulled so close to the dash that even Houdini would've struggled to squeeze in. Nervous driver, no doubt, but trying her best to act cool.

What really threw me off, though, was how chirpy she seemed, considering the mess we'd just walked away from this morning. Almost suspiciously upbeat. Relieved, even—more than I was, if that's possible. She talked with this quiet twinkle in her eyes and that half-smile, just crooked enough to be cute. It was the kind of smile that made you wonder if she knew more than she was letting on.

"Not sure, really," I said, smiling instinctively, the kind of smile that came unbidden whenever I talked to Julia. "Might pop 'round and give Billy some shit for ditching me last night."

In truth, I had no intention of doing that. I was still reeling from what happened—how someone had knocked me unconscious without me seeing it coming. The whole thing was a blur, and the more I thought about it, the less sense it made. I knew I needed answers. I just didn't have the first clue where to start.

Julia was having none of it.

"I think it'd be better if you gave it a few days before you reached out to Billy," she said, her voice gentle but firm. "Sure, call him—let him know what happened—but if the police are still watching you, you don't want to pull Billy into this, do you?" "You told me his dad's an arsehole. And you're both underage, so if anyone finds out you were drinking… Well, you could land him in even more trouble."

Good point! Underage drinking hadn't even crossed my mind.

"Yeah, you're probably right, as usual. Oh, and it's left here," I said, doing that ridiculous pointy thing like she didn't know which side was left.

The thing is, she was already signaling to turn, which threw me for a loop. She hadn't been to my flat in two years, so how the hell did she remember the way? I decided not to offer any more directions—no point pretending I was useful. Sure enough, she pulled up right outside, smooth as if she came by every week.

But the weirdest part? She found a parking spot right under the entrance. The knob head from the next flat had actually moved his massive Transit van. That thing hadn't budged in months.

Yeah, this was shaping up to be one seriously weird day.

"Here we are then," Julia said while mounting the curb with her front wheel to get into the space like that was the most natural thing ever. "Are you going to invite me in then for a coffee?"

I could see she was half joking, but the fact that she'd already turned off the engine suggested that maybe she wasn't. Oh, what the hell. I probably needed the company anyway and couldn't quite think of an excuse fast enough that wouldn't sound like I was politely telling her to leave me alone.

I gave her a big beaming smile and said, "Of course! As long as you don't mind drinking from a chipped mug. And remember, you have to be gentle with me; I'm not just a piece of meat!"

She laughed out loud, already out of the car before her seatbelt had even snapped back into place. I'd meant to do the whole gentlemanly thing—go around and open her door—but there I was, still wrestling with my own seatbelt like a rookie.

With a glance around the quiet street, we climbed the three worn stone steps to the front door of what must've once been a fancy house—before someone chopped it into bedsits. The place still clung to some old-world charm, but you could tell it had seen better days.

As we reached the door, I patted down my pockets, trying to find my key. It was always in my front left pocket—always. But of course, today was different. It hit me suddenly: the key was in the bag I was holding, along with the rest of my personal belongings.

Julia clearly found the spectacle highly amusing.

"So, how many cats should I expect when we finally get up there?" she jokingly asked.

The front door closed behind us, and I gestured to the stairs.

"After you, Ma'am."

The door to my first-floor bedsit never provided a good first impression. The paint was peeling off to the extent that you couldn't tell what the topcoat was and what the undercoat was. Despite telling the landlord on numerous occasions, he clearly didn't give a shit since every tenant's door looked the same. I'd stopped asking some months back.

Julia didn't seem to notice or was too polite to say anything, but I saw her genuine surprise when I opened the door.

Although the bedsit was small, the inside was immaculate; everything was in its place and spotlessly clean. Perhaps because I was a 17-year-old living alone, she expected a pigsty, which had been an apt description when I first moved in. She was supposed to visit me daily, then later weekly, as part of her role as my case worker, but she soon stopped after the first two weeks. Because the visits were very restrictive to my lifestyle, I never complained. I liked my own company.

"Make yourself at home." I gestured to the sofa and walked to the kitchenette, aware that the sofa was the only seat in the room. However, Julia was ahead of me and beat me to the kitchenette, opening one of the only two cupboards and searching for cups.

"I wasn't joking about the coffee," she said. "Be a love and put the kettle on."

Having produced two unmatching mugs, she walked up behind me while I filled the kettle and placed her warm hands on the back of my neck. All the hairs stood in appreciation of the warmth.

"Let's get this bandage off. I know those stitches must be pissing you off."

I instinctively went on the defensive, turning to tell her I was fine. But she pivoted with me, already untying the knot of the bandage, and I was stuck, kettle in hand, unable to stop her. In a flash, the bandage was undone, and she loosened it from around my neck and shoulder, exposing the stitches beneath.

"See, I was right," she exclaimed. "They must be really itchy with the wound having closed up so quickly. If you've got some scissors or a sharp knife, I can have them out in a jiffy". I spun around too quickly, and the overfilled kettle sprayed her jacket and the opening of her blouse. Just as I opened my mouth to offer some half-hearted excuse about why my wound had healed so quickly, the words never left my lips.

Julia burst out with a small laugh. "Really, Nathan, this isn't a porn film. Spraying my top with water won't make me take it off! At least not straight away!" She gave me a cheeky little wink and that smile before grabbing a handful of kitchen roll and dabbing off the water.

I must admit, that did make me laugh out loud and distracted me momentarily from trying to explain my wound.

"So, have you still got enough water in there for that coffee you promised? Or do I just die of thirst here?" She walked over to the sofa before dropping onto it and demurely crossing her legs. I decided to take advantage of the distraction and busy myself with the coffee.

"Do you want a biscuit or anything?" I asked, trying to remember if I actually had any.

Julia leaned forward, propping herself up to gaze out the window at the block of flats across the street. "No, I'm fine, thanks. Just one sweetener, if you have it, and a splash of milk. If not, I'll take it with just the milk."

Fortunately, I had a sweetener tucked away among a small pile of sachets I'd clearly pilfered from some fast-food joint. I hoped she wouldn't notice—and thankfully, it seemed she didn't. Just as I gathered everything needed to make the coffee, the kettle's switch popped up. I walked over with just Julia's mug, having decided to play the gentleman and stay in the kitchen. Julia would have none of that.

"Where's your mug? You can sit with me, you know. I won't bite." She patted the sofa beside her, doing that amusing little shuffle where she pretended to make room but didn't actually budge an inch. What the hell—might as well dive in. I retrieved my mug and strolled over, settling next to her with my right knee slightly angled onto the sofa between us. It was a friendly gesture, half-facing her while still maintaining a bit of space.

Julia took a sip of her coffee while looking directly in front of her before turning to face me directly. Without any emotion, she asked me a question that completely threw me off guard.

"So, Nathan Cartwright. Tell me who and what you really are."

Chapter 4

She's a Keeper

Sometimes life hits you with a curveball so unexpected, that it's like the whole world pauses for a second, just to watch you stumble. Did I see it coming? Not a chance. I was grasping at straws, looking for anything—any clue—that might ease the knot tightening in my chest. But for the first time since I'd known her, Julia's eyes were a locked door. No flicker of guilt, no softening around the edges, nothing. Just... silence.

Was she joking? Maybe a clumsy attempt at flirting?

Time was not on my side—if I waited too long, she'd know she hit a nerve. And yeah, she had, but I wasn't about to let her see that. I'd been down this road before. Moments like this were a game of poker, and I'd mastered the art of bluffing—whether by laying on the charm or acting like I didn't have a clue.

Opting for the charm offensive, I broke into a smile.

"Well, if you don't know that, then perhaps you're not really cut out to be a social worker." I raised my coffee cup and offered a "cheer" in an attempt to lighten the situation.

She matched my salutation with her own "cheers," theatrically raising her cup and bowing her head before revealing her warm smile. Phew! Maybe I'd read too much into it after all!

I hadn't.

After taking a sip of her coffee, which, by the barely hidden grimace, was either still too hot or, more likely, wasn't good, Julia did a quick look around to see where she could put the cup down.

"Don't worry about the lack of coasters. I'm not that sophisticated. Anywhere will do."

Julia's eyes scanned the room with purpose, and when she spotted what she needed, she slipped into the kitchenette. A moment later, she reappeared with a sheet of kitchen roll, folding it neatly in half before placing it under her cup.

"Nonsense," she said, settling back into the sofa. This time, she shifted to face me fully, her left leg tucked comfortably beneath her. "Hot cups always leave marks on nice wood."

Without missing a beat, her hand drifted onto mine, resting lightly on the back of the sofa. On any other day, I might've read too much into the touch, searching for meaning. But the slight widening of her deep blue eyes told me everything—romance wasn't even on her radar. Whatever she had to say, it was building inside her, and it mattered.

I wasn't wrong.

"You kind of hit the nail on the head, Nathan. I know you were perhaps joking when you said I wasn't much of a social worker, but the thing is, you're right." She gave a slight, apologetic bow.

I immediately tried to console her, lightly gripping her hand before releasing it and using my right forefinger to gently raise her chin in an attempt to look into her eyes.

"Nonsense, you're the best," I said in a soft voice.

Sliding her hand down the back of the sofa and sitting up straight, she seemed to regain her business-like composure suddenly.

"No. You see, I need to tell you something. It's something I should have told you, perhaps when I first met you, but couldn't for various reasons."

Realizing that she was really struggling and, to be honest, having no idea where the conversation was going, I consciously leaned back into a less confrontational and relaxed position on the sofa.

"Hey, just take your time. I'm actually a very good listener."

My comment drew a wistful little smirk, the kind that might have blossomed into a real smile if not for the nerves holding it back. She reached for her coffee, crossed her legs with quiet grace, and wrapped both hands around the mug like a shield. For a moment, she just held my gaze, steady and unflinching, as if gathering herself. Then, with a deep breath, she began her story.

"Firstly, Nathan, I'm not actually your social worker. Well, not officially, that is. I'm actually what's known as your Keeper."

I started to ask what she meant, but she put her forefinger to her mouth.

"Look, this is going to be hard enough for me, so please just let me get it all out. There will be plenty of time for your questions later."

She seemed almost frightened, so I nodded and gave a wink, which drew a quick but nervous smile.

"Don't get me wrong, I am a social worker, but you're not actually on the Council's books. You're not a 'case,' so to speak. I was given the task to 'look after you.'" A point she emphasized by doing little speech marks with both hands. "That's why, after the few visits following your arrival, I've never been back. I didn't need to because, as far as your landlord is concerned, you're actually 19 and not 17. That's what first got me intrigued!"

She waited for me to respond, but I needed to know exactly how much she knew, so I raised both eyebrows in mock surprise and motioned for her to continue. She seemed to grow in confidence the more she spoke, and I didn't want to interrupt her flow.

"You see, all I've been told is that your parents both died in an accident when you were young, and you were left with a considerable amount of money. So, why a bedsit? Do you still have all the money they left for you? Why are you still in the sixth form at school? These are all questions I've been meaning to ask for some time but was told not to. However, being a 'girl'…" She winked to remind me it was a stereotype. "I'm inherently a nosey bitch, so I started visiting your school as your Social Worker."

I had no idea about the school visits. "Why? If you don't mind me asking. It's not as if I've ever been in trouble there…"

"On the contrary, you're the model student by all accounts, and your grades are superb. This is surprising because when I looked in your locker—oh, I used the drugs excuse to the Head—you take very little notes in class, and you never use a laptop. So, you're either some kind of genius or something else entirely. And it's that something else I'd like to know about."

"But why? I mean, why now? It all sounds very James Bond. I'm starting to feel a little special!"

"Ah, but you are special, Nathan, and I know that because that's what I was told when I took you on. Initially, I thought it was just a term of endearment, but now realize it's something else entirely."

She took both of my hands in hers and looked directly into my eyes.

"You see, today will be the last day I will ever see you, and you know I've always liked you so much. And who knows, perhaps if I'd

22

known a little more about you, it may have gone further." She blushed a bit.

Her confession caught me off guard. Any other time, I might've tried to take advantage of the moment—after all, I'd been with other women before. But none of them had left a mark the way Julia had. Love? I wasn't sure. But something about her stirred feelings I wasn't used to—something warm, steady, and safe. And the thought of losing her hit harder than I expected.

"But why?" I asked. "I mean, why do you have to quit?"

"It's not my choice, Nathan. You see, the person who employs me pays me an awful lot of money, far more than my official social worker job. They're relocating me to Swindon to look after someone apparently very like you. So, what I'm asking you, as a friend, and I hope that we'll still be friends, is… What *is* a 'someone like you?' I know there's an awful lot about you I don't know, but it must be something special if someone is prepared to go to these lengths to make sure you're okay. So, going back to my original question, Nathan: Who are you? What are you?"

I suppose this was always going to come sometime, but even so, it still surprised me. You see, normally, I would have gone on the defensive straight away, but something held me back. I really cared for Julia, and if this was to be her chosen career path, I felt it was fair for her to know what she would be dealing with.

I stood and gathered our coffee cups, carrying them into the kitchen. After setting them in the sink, I reached into the cupboard for two matching crystal brandy glasses and the bottle of Hardy Perfection—no ordinary drink. Retailing at around £18,000 a bottle, though it had cost me far less at the time. I doubted Julia would notice the difference, but that didn't matter. If this was going to be the end, I figured I might as well go out with a bang.

23

"I think we're going to need something a little stronger if you want me to tell you everything, so this may help."

I returned to the sofa and placed her glass on the coffee table directly in front of her. However, instead of sitting next to her, I took a few steps back and leaned against the kitchenette worktop. I raised my glass to say cheers, but this time, although she raised her glass in response, she didn't say anything.

Maintaining eye contact, I started with a smile to let her know everything would be all right. It must have helped because she sat back on the sofa and tried to smile back.

"Okay, Julia. Since you asked, I'm going to tell you all about me. But only because I do genuinely care for you and think you should know. However, be warned; it's a long story, and in places, you may think I'm talking utter bullshit. I will, however, try to explain everything, and by the end, hopefully, you'll see how it all fits together. All I ask is that you never, ever, no matter what the occasion, repeat what I'm about to tell you to anyone. And I mean *anyone*. Do you understand?"

I'd definitely caught her full attention. Her eyes flickered around the room as if she were either looking for someone who may be listening in or trying to figure out an escape. She then looked directly at me and took a sip of her brandy.

"Don't worry. I've already strapped myself in, as I guessed it may be a bumpy ride. And don't worry about me saying anything to anyone; I guarantee whatever you tell me will be just between the two of us." She gave a genuine smile.

"And I believe you. However, if you could just take your phone out and place it on the table, I'd appreciate it. I know you won't be recording this, but you have to understand that if anything I'm about

24

to tell you did get out, I'd be in grave danger."

She duly rummaged about in her bag and produced her phone, which she then switched to silent.

"Okay, then, Julia. Let's enlighten you."

Chapter 5

Dispelling a Few Myths

I took a deep breath. "First of all, and you've probably guessed this by now, I'm not actually 17. I'm 115 years old—about to turn 116."

I wasn't sure what kind of reaction I was expecting from Julia. A gasp? Widened eyes? Maybe a laugh? But I got none of that. She simply kept her gaze fixed over the top of her brandy glass, then lowered it slightly, as if she was about to say something but decided against it. Did she mishear me?

"You see, I was born in 1908, just after the turn of the last century."

"But how?" Julia ran her fingers through her neat bob, messing up the perfectly maintained parting and nearly spilling her brandy.

"It might be better if you put that down," I suggested with a light laugh.

"So, what are you then? Some kind of zombie? A vampire? I mean, how..." She gestured with her palms facing upward, waiting for an answer that matched her confusion.

I knew exactly what she meant—she was on the right track.

"Look," I said, "I know this is a lot to take in—probably more than a bit. But if you want the full story, you'll need to listen. It's a long one, but I promise by the end, you'll understand. Then, I'll answer any questions you might have."

I took a sip of the fine brandy—if I do say so myself—set the glass on the worktop and walked over to sit on the edge of the coffee table, just inches from her face. The good thing was, she didn't flinch. Instead, she crossed her legs and leaned back on the sofa.

"Sorry. I mean, yes; go on, and I'll try and stay quiet, which, as you know, may be hard for me!" She gave a nervous smile.

Good, at least she wasn't too freaked out and still had that sense of humor I loved about her.

I took another deep breath and then began to tell her about my life, maintaining eye contact to gauge any adverse reactions or warning signs.

"You see, you were nearly right in what you said about the vampire thing—although I personally don't like that term. I'm sure you've seen that film 'Interview with a Vampire.'"

This elicited a faint nod of recognition.

"Well, forget everything about it! Personally, it did people like me—oh, yes, there are others—a massive favor as it cemented people's perceptions of what a Vampire is. But as you'll see throughout my story, it couldn't be further from the truth. Anyway, I digress; let's go back to the beginning.

"As I mentioned, I was born in 1908, the first and only child of Wilfred and Mary Cartwright. Nathan Cartwright is actually my birth name! And it may surprise you to hear this, but we were quite poor, living hand to mouth. My father was, quite literally, a cartwright—he repaired and built carts in the small country village where we lived in Surrey.

"That's the first of many myths I'm about to dispel. Vampires are rarely nobility living in grand estates. Think about it—before the first of the great wars, most people, especially in rural areas, weren't very well educated, if at all. Back then, people were executed for being suspected witches, and even handicapped babies would regularly 'go missing.' So why would anyone like us want to draw attention by posing as the Lord of the Manor?

"No, the survival of my kind over the centuries has been entirely dependent on blending into society."

"Oh, and just so you know, you don't turn into a vampire by being bitten. It's actually genetic. If either your father or mother is a vampire, there's a good chance you'll become one, too. Even then, you don't *grow up* as a vampire. And by the way, I'm only using the term *vampire* because it's the one you're familiar with. Personally, I hate it. Hollywood has ruined the word, associating it with violence and death, which couldn't be further from the truth. I was born a vampire."

I hesitated for a moment, then added with a reassuring smile, "Oh, and I should mention—you're perfectly safe. But I'm guessing you've realized that by now."

"You probably also think that vampires need fresh blood to survive and need it regularly, and that also isn't true. Yes, we do need blood or, to be more specific, the iron contained within it. And I must admit, the vampire films and series, whether by accident or research, nearly got this right. Think of a vampire from the TV or Cinema who needs to feed, and you'll probably picture a creature that seems tired and weak, with pale, cold skin and brittle nails. Now, guess what? Humans who have an iron deficiency display the exact same symptoms. Yes, all the same symptoms. So, you see, we're not that different from you!

"Although I didn't realize it at the time when I was born—before I even suckled my mother's milk—I was given a muslin cloth soaked in the blood from birth to suck on. If you think about it, it's not so different from the animal world. Many female animals eat the placenta after birth to regain their strength—it's an excellent source of iron.

"In addition to my mother's milk, we also drank the blood of animals my father brought home from his hunts: rabbits, hares, and occasionally, even a stray cat. Back then, people in the countryside didn't often buy food; they ate whatever they could find or catch. My father would slit the animals' throats before hanging them to cure, and we would drink the blood."

"Unfortunately, my mother died when I was seven after contracting an infection after being kicked by a horse. That was the first time I'd experienced real emotion."

Julia stood to slip off her shoes and remove her jacket. She pressed both shoulders back in an effort to get her arms out of the sleeves. Her silk blouse was under tremendous pressure from those boobs clearly encased in what was a frilly black bra. Bloody, magnificent, and far bigger than I had imagined.

"Whoa, I don't get it," she said as she folded her jacket, carefully laying it over the arm of the chair. "It's the aging thing I don't get."

She started to walk around the coffee table, and my mind started thinking about what she could be doing. Option 1: she grabs one of her four-inch stilettos and tries to brain me with it. That was hardly likely since she was only a slip of a thing. I really hoped it was Option 2, where she felt so relaxed that she'd walk over, drape her arms around my neck, feel sorry for me, and start passionately kissing me.

Unfortunately, it turned out to be Option 3. She walked over to the window, running her fingers through her hair as she gazed down at the two kids from downstairs kicking a ball around the street. Every

29

now and then, the ball would thud against a parked car, but no one seemed to care. The kids were having fun, and no harm was done. It was a quiet neighborhood, which suited me just fine.

"I mean, how do you not get noticed? You're apparently over a hundred years old, yet you look like you haven't even hit twenty. How do people not notice that?"

"Ah, so you *are* paying attention. And that, my dear, is a very good question!"

Feeling more at ease with how calmly she was handling the conversation, I decided to pour myself another brandy. There was no need to ask if she wanted a refill—she wasn't even halfway through her first glass. That made sense. She seemed more like a spritzer kind of girl, probably too young to appreciate the smooth, rich taste of a fine brandy.

"You see, that's another thing the movies never get right. So, ten out of ten for noticing. I have to admit, it's a strange process. For the first seven years of life, we age just like anyone else, no different from you. But after that, things get... sketchy. Around the age of seven, we stop aging in the usual sense. How long we stay the same 'age' depends on other factors, which I'll explain later. In my case, I stopped aging—and no, it wasn't because of my mother's death; that was just a bad coincidence. That's when my father had to give me up to the Fayre people."

Julia glanced over her shoulder, her voice incredulous. "Your dad gave you to the Fayre? Why?"

She turned fully and returned to the sofa, this time sitting on the edge, leaning forward, her chin resting in her hands, elbows on her knees. She was definitely hooked.

I decided to press on, aware that at this pace, it would take all evening to finish my story. And although she seemed more relaxed, I doubted she had any intention of staying the night. I mentally scolded myself for imagining what it would be like if she did.

"It wasn't like that," I quickly added, raising my hand as if offering an apology on my father's behalf. "You see, back then, it was quite common for my kind to join a fayre or circus. If you've ever been to a fayre, you've probably looked at the travelers and wondered, 'Why would anyone want to live like this?' I mean, aside from the attention of teenage girls, it's hardly a glamorous life. But what you might not have realized is that there were likely a few of my kind among the troupe.

"You probably wouldn't have noticed them—they were mostly kids, not the charming lotharios who jump onto the back of your dodgem trying to impress you. Although, to be fair, a few of those guys are part of my kind, too."

"Think about it. You're constantly moving around the country from week to week, so unless you visit the circus or fayre and take particular note of a person, and then attend again in a few years when the circus or fayre returns, you're unlikely to notice the person hadn't seemed to age.

"You may also have read or seen on the media about people going missing when the circus or fayre visits—yes, fayres are now more popular than circuses but serve the same purpose. 'They must have run off to join the Fayre.' Funnily enough, these cases rarely seem to attract the attention of the police or media, which I personally think is sad. I also feel partly guilty for this since nine times out of ten, it was one of my kind that killed them for blood—something I definitely don't approve of, by the way." I held my hands up in an apology.

Julia grimaced slightly and stood. "So, how is it you don't look seven? Why do you look older?"

31

I flipped around and took her seat on the sofa, resting my long legs on the coffee table. Okay, I still had my shoes on, but hey, it was my flat, so I could do what I wanted. I was about to respond when she walked towards me from the window. It couldn't have happened at a better time! The sun was directly behind her, slowly sinking into the sky, which made her blouse effectively transparent, leaving her curves clearly visible. My God, she was hot!

She carefully removed her folded jacket and laid it on the coffee table as if she feared me creasing it. But then, she pulled the only cushion (why would I need more than one living alone) and positioned it against the arm of the sofa before sitting down next to me.

Flinging her legs across mine and twisting to face me, she casually said, as if it were the most natural thing in the world, "You don't mind rubbing my feet, do you? I mean, heels are cute, but wearing them all day really takes its toll. You don't mind, right?"

I could feel the heat rising in my face, knowing I was blushing, but I decided to play it cool—going full macho like it was something I'd been asked to do a thousand times. Mentally, I told myself to grow up and stop acting like a lovestruck schoolboy.

"Sure," I said and started to gently massage her beautifully manicured feet like I actually knew what the hell I was doing. "Sorry, what was the question again?"

"I said, why don't you look seven anymore? I mean, how do you look so old? Don't get me wrong," she said, smiling sweetly. "I don't mean old, but you're clearly not seven!"

I laughed genuinely, though I wasn't quite sure how, given that I was still concentrating on massaging her feet, trying not to come across as the complete amateur I clearly was.

She closed her eyes for a moment and murmured, "Mmmm,

that's lovely."

It was a tricky question to answer, mainly because I didn't really know the answer myself. I had an idea, though, based on something I was told once by someone at the Fayre. Since I didn't have a better explanation, I figured I'd share what little I knew with Julia.

"I think it's triggered by some sort of strong emotion," I began. "I say 'think' because I'm not entirely certain. It's only happened to me once—back in 1947. Although I hated the life of a traveler, with the hard work and constant moving, they treated me like the family I never had. I got to travel the country, and during tough times, especially throughout both World Wars, they always made sure I had enough to sustain me."

I was expecting a reaction to the word sustenance from Julia. I mean. I could have just said *food*, but I was trying to be honest. Although she didn't show any visible change in emotion—perhaps because of the quality of the foot massage—I sensed a quickening in her heartbeat. Either way, I was about to continue when Julia stopped me.

"I don't get why you didn't get involved with either of the wars. I mean, with all that bloodshed, there must have been lots of sustenance available."

"You have to understand," I said while trying to look as much like a persecuted individual as possible by dipping my eyes and focusing on her feet, which wasn't as difficult as it sounded since the foot massage had already developed into a foot/ankle/lower leg massage. "The only way our people have survived so long is by keeping a low profile. You have to remember that every time some bloody Vampire film, story or series is released, people, whether consciously or unconsciously, become more aware of their surroundings. Couple that with the fear and anxiety of warfare, and that makes it very precarious for the likes of us. No, far better to be a seven-year-old helping out at the fayre."

Julia pulled her feet away abruptly, drawing her knees up to her chest and wrapping her arms around them in what I could only assume was a defensive posture.

"You still haven't told me how you changed from a seven-year-old into a… Whatever you are now."

Perhaps she was right to adopt a more defensive posture; perhaps she anticipated what I was about to tell her.

"Well, this is what I remember," I began. "Like I said, I think it's triggered by strong emotions—you know, that fight-or-flight response when the adrenaline really kicks in. It started, I think, one weekend during a Fayre somewhere in Lancashire—I can't remember exactly where. It was a relatively busy weekend. People were still celebrating the end of the war, and, being Lancashire, of course, it was raining. Most people were huddled around the stalls and rides, looking for some shelter.

"I wasn't allowed to mingle, being only seven at the time. That could've drawn too much attention. Instead, I was tasked with fetching and carrying supplies for the stall owners. That Saturday evening, I came out of the supply tent, holding some homemade preserves, when I heard a low groaning sound coming from between our tent and the one next to it. Curious, I set the jars down and moved into the shadows to investigate. And that's when I saw her."

"She was probably in her early twenties—a 'large-boned' young woman, lying face down with her floral dress bunched up around her waist. Blood was trickling from her mouth, forming bubbles every time she tried to cry out, which came out more like groaning and gurgling sounds. That's when I noticed the tip of a tent peg, barely visible in the dark. It blended with the deep red blood pouring from a wound in her stomach.

"I quickly glanced around and realized we were completely alone. I could only imagine that she had come here for some privacy, maybe to relieve herself, and had slipped in the mud, falling onto the tent peg and impaling herself. Her heart was racing... And then my life changed forever. I'll tell you now—I'm not proud of what happened next.

"You see, I could have saved her. I could have run for help, shouted, or done something. But I didn't. All I could see was the blood seeping out."

"You killed her?" Julia asked with incredulity. Her eyes were wide, and whether she knew it or not, her jaw hung open.

"No, no. I mean, I don't think so. She was certainly still alive, although unconscious when I left her. It was the blood, the smell, and, in hindsight, perhaps inexperience, but instead of helping her, I knelt and started to drink the blood from her wound. It tasted so good. So fresh."

My eyes began to water, unintentionally betraying the emotions I had tried to keep at bay. I turned to look Julia in the eyes, wiping a tear from my right eye with the sleeve of my shirt. My voice, now close to breaking, pressed on as best as it could.

"I actually went to the graveyard for her funeral. Not as a guest, of course—I just lingered out of sight, away from the main group. It wasn't until I saw what I assumed was her younger sister, bawling her eyes out while being held tightly by their mother, who was equally devastated, that the reality of it all truly hit me. There was no father there to comfort them, so I assumed, like many, he'd paid the ultimate price during the war.

"I could have helped. I could have run for help when I found

35

her. I could have at least held her in her final moments. But I didn't. Instead, I did nothing but satisfy my own urges. For the next two days, I cried myself to sleep, completely wrecked by guilt. My fellow Carnies seemed to understand, and someone was always with me, keeping watch. On the evening of the second day, they had a quiet conversation among themselves before giving me a warm potion to help me sleep.

"The next morning, I woke up feeling... strange. Turning to my right, still half-asleep, I noticed a pile of clothes on the caravan's only chair. They weren't mine—the trousers were far too long, and I didn't wear trousers. I always wore shorts. That's when I noticed my arms, and with a surge of panic, I ripped the sheet down to see the rest of my body. The scream I let out brought Mike rushing into the caravan, and strangely enough, he was smiling.

"And that, you see, is when I became what you see now."

Julia stared at me, unblinking. I could see her eyes darting rapidly, not really focused on me but rather lost in her thoughts, trying to process everything.

In one fluid movement, she spun around, resting her left arm on the back of the sofa. She leaned into me with her shoulder, tucking her legs up onto the cushion, almost like young lovers cozying up to watch a movie. Then, gently tussling the back of my hair without looking at me, she said, "Oh, you poor thing. That must have been awful. And that poor girl... her mother... how do you ever get over something like that?"

Maybe it was because I had let a genuine tear fall, but never in my long life had anyone offered me such comfort. I could feel the warmth of her body against mine, her perfume subtly filling the air. I noticed her heartbeat—calm, far more relaxed than I had anticipated.

As she slowly turned her head to look at me, I took the

opportunity to slide my right arm, which had been awkwardly pinned between us, onto the back of the sofa, careful not to touch her.

"Sorry," I said, sensing she may think I was getting a little too cozy with her. "I just needed to get a little more comfortable, and my arm was pinned—"

"It's okay. She smiled a sweet smile. "Well, you've already done my feet, so I wouldn't say no if you offered to give me a little head massage."

I couldn't tell if she was joking or not, so I responded in mock servitude. "Well, of course, Ma'am." I gently started to run my fingers through her hair.

Should I take this moment to kiss her? God, I so wanted to! I'd probably never get a better chance, but I was snapped out of it with another question.

"So, what happened then? I mean, one moment you're seven, and the next day you're... Well, you're like you are now. Surely, the other Fayre people realized."

"Oh, they did, but it was all of a bit of a haze. They'd only just gotten rid of the police, who thankfully recognized the death as an accident. Still, Carnie people are never too keen on any form of investigation by any authority, so the decision had been to strip down and move on earlier than planned. And then, of course, there was me, suddenly viewing the world from two feet higher than before, which I can tell you is a pretty weird experience. It was only after the second or third person had called me Nathan that I realized that life would go on as though nothing had happened. It was then that Mike told me they had seen this type of thing before, and in the carnie, you never ask awkward questions. So, in the end, we moved on, and life carried on as it was right through to the mid-70s."

37

"So, what happened then, Nathan? I mean, why leave the Fayre when it was obvious people there knew who, I mean, what you were? Sorry, that sounds really awful, but I'm still trying to get used to it."

I didn't look at her as I didn't want to spoil the moment of intimacy and cause her to move, so I continued stroking her hair and gave her an honest answer.

"I got bored. Plus, you have to remember that I had to prepare myself for life. I'd never been to school but could read and write thanks to Mike, and even if I say so myself, it turns out I'm quite intelligent!"

"Oh, I know that." She laughed. "Remember, I've seen your school records."

"Anyway, I needed to make money of my own now that I looked old enough to work. 'Fairground Operative' doesn't exactly stand out as a sparkling reference! I did some laboring, moving from site to site with different companies, and through contacts, I began my first apprenticeship as a joiner. My employer was a guy called Jim Mason, which I thought was amusing with him being a joiner. I was actually very good at it, but remember I used to work as a Wright mending and building carts as a youngster, and despite it being many years ago, I still remember it like yesterday.

"You're probably wondering how I could afford to live and where the money comes from. Well, let me try to clear that up for you now. I say try because I'm not 100% sure how it works myself. You see, back in the Carnie days, Mike always looked after me, and for some reason, he never seemed to be short of money despite his stall seemingly only making a pittance. However, as I said earlier, those are the sort of questions you never ask Carnie folk. Anyway, when I was leaving, he told me I had a trust fund—whatever the hell one of those was—set up by my father and that someone would always pay accommodation costs until I got 'older.' I know that still happens to-day. I don't pay rent here, but I have no idea who does. And, of course, a 17-year-old asking the landlord who pays rent is probably not the best way to stay out of sight, out of mind, so I just live with it."

Julia looked up at me as if about to say something. She tried to form the first word, but something clearly changed her mind. Instead, she moved on to my dietary requirements. "I'm sorry, Nathan. I've been meaning to ask this for a while now, and please don't take it the wrong way. Do you kill people to drink their blood?" She blushed as if she was embarrassed to have even asked. Her heartbeat sped up—per-haps in anticipation of bad news or even fear. "Don't worry." I gently squeezed her shoulder for reassurance. "You're perfectly safe if that's what you're worried about. No, I haven't and never will. You see, I don't need to kill, but to understand why, I'll need to go into more detail."

Chapter 6

I'd Like to Phone a Friend

"Tell you what," Julia said, glancing at her watch. "Do you mind if I call a work colleague first? We're supposed to hook up tonight for a night out, and I just want to inform them that I'll be a little late."

I'm not sure what expression crossed my face—probably surprise. I'd honestly thought she might stay the night. But I was wrong.

"Don't worry, Nathan," she said with a teasing, almost condescending look. "It's just a girlfriend!"

I laughed, mostly out of relief.

She walked over to the window, then turned to face me, holding her phone close to her chest. Tilting her head to one side in a mockingly playful way, she watched me.

"Do you mind?"

At first, I had no idea what she meant. Talk about acting like a 17-year-old!

"Of course. I need to use the bathroom anyway. That brandy seems to have gone right through me." It hadn't, of course, but in a small bedsit, the only other room with any privacy was the bathroom. So I got up and strolled over, glancing back over my shoulder.

"Now, don't you go running off."

She laughed. "Don't worry. If I were going to make a break for

40

it, don't you think I'd have done it already—especially after everything you've told me? I'll still be here, and if not, well, you've got my jacket and shoes as hostage!" She flashed a beaming smile that lit up her face.

I switched on the bathroom light and closed the door behind me. I tried to catch what Julia was saying, but her words were drowned out as soon as the light flicked on—the extraction fan came to life, humming loudly and adding an annoying clicking sound, likely from the fan catching the casing. It had never bothered me before.

I waited until Julia's voice faded, then went through the motions of flushing and running the tap for a few seconds. When I stepped out, she was already back on the sofa, settled in her familiar sideways position with her knees tucked beneath her. She patted the cushion beside her with her left hand, inviting me to sit close again. Maybe all wasn't lost after all.

"Everything sorted?" I asked.

"Absolutely! She was actually very understanding and even joked that it must be a hot boy holding me up from finishing work on a weekend this late! I told her it might be…" She gave me a cheeky wink.

Before I could think of anything flirtatious to say, Julia jumped straight back to the subject.

"So, you were saying that you don't kill to feed… How do you survive? Where do you get your blood supplies? Do you kill animals? Oh my God, don't tell me you kill family pets?" she asked with a look of genuine horror.

"No, no! It's nothing like that." I held up my hands defensively. "Let me explain! As I said before, we suffer from a lack of iron that we can only get from iron-rich blood. For some reason, medications and iron supplements don't work. I don't know why; they just don't. So, once in a while, we have to drink blood. Animal blood can help in a pinch, but it can cause long-term damage if relied on. Think of it like eating only burgers or bacon sandwiches—they'll satisfy you for a while, but if that's all you ate, you'd eventually become diabetic or suffer heart failure."

"We do try and stave it off. If you look in my cupboards, you'll see a lot of iron-rich foods such as red meat, spinach, peas, beetroot juice, etc. However, the bottom line is that every now and again, we need human blood, and no, we don't steal bags of plasma from hospitals like you may have read or seen in the movies because they too make no difference."

"So, if you have to feed on humans, how do you do it? I mean, you don't even have fangs," Julia said, unconsciously pointing to her mouth as if I might not know what fangs were. "And how come the place isn't littered with blood-drained corpses?"

I burst out laughing. "There you go again, leaning on the good ol' movie stereotypes. I mean, I don't even have a cape! As I said before, movies actually did my kind favor by pushing that image—the wealthy old aristocrat sleeping in a coffin, draining virgins with razor-sharp fangs. Just think about it for a second. Fangs usually mean canines, right? So, how would you go through life hiding them? In the movies, they just pop out as if they're retractable! And then there's Stephen King's Salem's Lot, with Mr. Barlow sporting fangs in the front like Nosferatu. That actually scared me the first time I saw it, but again, those fangs couldn't be further from reality."

"I do, actually, have what you call fangs." Julia's eyes momentarily widened.

"They're actually at the back. Calling them fangs is probably misleading. It's the front edge of the upper and lower molars—they're raised, razor-sharp, and angled backward." I decided it wasn't the best idea to show Julia, so I continued explaining instead.

"Think about it—if we stick to the movie stereotype, anyone faced with a vampire wouldn't just give in; they'd fight like hell, and that could easily lead to a fang getting ripped out. But having them on a molar lets you grip without tearing. If done right, the person might not even realize they've been bitten." Julia looked ready to ask another question, so I quickly added, "But I'll get to that in a minute."

"We're not alone in this peculiar quirk of nature. The Eastern Hognose snake in North America has developed similarly to us. Although relatively harmless, its venom isn't strong enough to hurt humans, and unlike other venomous snakes that strike when threatened, the Hognose will first flatten its head to imitate a Cobra. If that doesn't work, it will flip on its back and writhe around pretending to be dead because predators won't usually attack an animal that looks like it's dying. That's the same with us and you. I mean, would you eat a fish found washed up on a beach? Probably not, as you don't know what it died from. The Hognose snake's fangs are actually at the back of its mouth, like us, and are used for popping the toads it eats—toads inflate themselves when threatened to make them harder to swallow."

Julia listened intently, and I could tell she still had plenty of questions. It could be a long night, and I secretly hoped it would be. Her body language reassured me—she didn't see me as a threat, and the personal nature of what I was sharing seemed to create a bond between us. I assumed it was because she realized I didn't go around telling just anyone. I think it made her feel a bit special. She was, at least to me.

"So, if you don't kill humans…" She made a circular motion with her hand to indicate that I needed to keep moving on with the story.

"Okay, this is going to sound a bit gross, but hear me out. And remember, however sick it may sound, think what the alternative could be. All I'm saying is, please don't judge me. It's a need I have, not some sort of fetish."

She sat up and to my surprise, lightly patted my arm. In a re-assuring voice, she said, "Just take your time. I know this isn't easy for you, and I'm probably the least judgmental person you'll ever meet." She smiled warmly. "I really appreciate you trusting me with this, and I promise I won't let you down."

I instinctively knew she was being sincere. Taking a deep breath, I prepared myself for what was coming next—the hardest part.

"I do feed from females, so, in a way, that *is* like in the movies, but the only reason is because it's easier. However, the difference is, that they're consenting adults, and I don't need to put them in any sort of a trance. I can't actually do that, anyway. That's another myth. The choice of girl is crucial; it can't just be any female; she needs to have an excess of iron in her blood."

I could see the confusion on Julia's face. "I'm guessing you're about to ask, 'How do you know?'" I paused, searching for the right words. "I usually… well, I only approach—'target' isn't the best term, but it's the one that comes to mind right now—older women, typically around their 30s, who are a bit overweight and, if possible, diabetic. They're more likely to have Hemochromatosis, an excess of iron in their blood. When they do, they tend to wear heavy makeup to mask the bronze or greyish tone of their skin."

I chuckled slightly. "DI Green made me tingle back at the sta-tion, but let's be real—there's a time and place and a police station in-terview, isn't it!"

"The best hunting grounds, so to speak, are the night clubs, and it's there that I go when I need to feed. They're usually easy to spot if you know what signs to look for, and the perfect one is one just about to come into her period." I looked into Julia's eyes to affirm honesty. "Yes, I can also sense that. Later on in the night, after they've usually had a few drinks, sometimes more than a few, so they're usually flattered when someone my age makes a pass at them.

"And of course, being a woman, they're usually out with other women, who most of the time are more attractive, so they have either already pulled or, if not, are pleased someone finds their friend attractive. Either way, it's not usually difficult to end up walking out of the club with your chosen lady. Whether they take me back to their place or we go back to mine, the result is usually the same: We end up sleeping together. However, none of the 'quickie' stuff for me; I always go down on the girl, and this is the key! You see, while down there, I gently pierce them with one of my special teeth—which 90% of the time they hardly feel, and if they do, I just say sorry as if it was an accident because any pain is over so quickly. So then, while doing my duty—so to speak—I'm also drinking. By the end, there is usually very little blood, and even if they do discover a little, they're hardly likely to mention it out of embarrassment.

"I usually leave shortly after because they tend to get quite tired. If you've ever given blood, you know the feeling. I suppose I could go all out and offer them a cup of tea and a biscuit afterward, but that might be pushing it!" I chuckled. "So, there you have it—no one gets hurt, and, honestly, they even enjoy themselves."

Julia now knew the truth, but she seemed unsure of how to respond. She looked down at her hands, then back at me, as if she was about to say something, then repeated the motion. The silence stretched on, almost deafening, making me wonder if I'd shared too much.

Then, suddenly, the buzzer rang, breaking the quiet.

Someone was at the building door requesting access to my bedsit.

Chapter 7

You say Hello, and I say Goodbye

I glanced at the buzzer, then back at Julia. "Well? Aren't you going to answer that, Nathan? Seems someone's rather eager to see you. That's the third time they've buzzed."

"Yeah, probably just someone trying to sell me something. Or a Jehovah's Witness—which won't be much use, considering their religion doesn't allow them to give blood!"

I stood up, thinking that was quite funny, but Julia just gave me what appeared to be a rather forced smile. As I moved toward the door, I said something banal like, "Don't go anywhere; I'll be back in a minute," immediately realizing how unoriginal it sounded. Still mulling over what I could've said to keep the mood light, I bounded down the steps, taking them two at a time.

I supposed I should've asked who it was, but I couldn't be bothered. All I wanted was to get rid of them and get back to Julia, hoping to lighten the mood I'd left her in. I opened the door with a few words already prepared, but the sight in front of me left me speechless.

"Hello, Nathan," said 'Does Nowt.' "Glad you're in; I thought you might've gone out for the evening."

I hadn't noticed the darkness setting in. "Detective." I couldn't quite remember how to pronounce her name correctly—and I definitely couldn't call her 'Does Nowt.'

"Oh, please, just call me Lucy," she said with a smile. "This is just an informal visit. I wanted to update you on the latest regarding the stabbing. Do you mind if I come in?" The question was rhetorical, as she was already stepping past me before finishing her sentence.

"I take it you're on the first floor, judging by the address," she said, already making her way up the stairs at a surprising pace, especially considering those designer heels with the red soles.

"Yeah, but I've actually got company…" I started to say.

"Oooh, female company, is it?" She glanced over her shoulder with a grin.

"Actually, it's my social worker, if you must know—"

"Well, that's even better. I can kill two birds with one stone and save myself another visit."

She stopped at the door, stepping aside politely to let me open it.

I opened the door, and once again, she breezed past me before I had a chance to react, strolling over to the couch Julia had vacated. Julia, having taken the time to put her shoes and jacket back on, was now standing in the kitchen, looking all formal—as if she, too, had just arrived. What struck me as particularly interesting was that she didn't seem the least bit surprised by Lucy's sudden entrance.

"Miss Featherstone," Lucy greeted. "Lucy Dunough. We met earlier today when we were chatting to Nathan." Instead of walking over to shake hands, Lucy sat down on the sofa without any invitation to do so. Something was clearly going on here that I wasn't aware of, and it was starting to cause the hair to rise on the back of my neck.

"So, Julia, what have you two been chatting about then? I thought you'd have gone home a long time ago…"

Although the question seemed innocent enough and was

delivered in a friendly tone, it clearly made Julia nervous.

"Oh, you know, nothing really. Just this and that," Julia replied. "I was actually just about to leave."

Lucy turned to face me. Whether by design or not, I had positioned myself in a neutral spot, careful not to stand closer to one than the other. She waved the back of her hand toward Julia, almost in a dismissive gesture.

"So, has Miss Featherstone told you yet that this will be the last time she'll see you?" Julia looked like she'd had the life slapped out of her. Lucy seemed to have some sort of hold over her. I remember Julia said she was moving away, but I never thought this would be the last time I'd see her. And how did Lucy know? Maybe it's a coincidence? Maybe I'd read too much into it.

I didn't get a chance to answer, which was a relief—I didn't want to compromise Julia in any way. Lucy's question must have been rhetorical because she carried on without waiting for a reply.

"Did she tell you she works for me?"

This caught me completely off guard. Julia's expression mirrored mine.

Julia was the first to speak, her voice betraying her surprise. "So, you're Mrs. Fanshaw?"

Lucy gave a brief, derogatory snigger. "Of course not, my Dear." She turned her focus to me. "You see, Miss Featherstone is paid to make sure you're okay, Nathan. And that you don't get into trouble, which I'm sure you'll agree was going very well until the last few days! However, I can't hold Miss Featherstone to blame for that; after all, boys will be boys!

"Anyway, Nathan, it's time to say your goodbyes to Miss

Featherstone." She turned to Julia and, with more than a drip of sarcasm, said, "I'm assuming you're still okay to drive?" She scooped up the empty brandy glass and sniffed it. "You've certainly got very good taste, Nathan. A shame it seems to be limited to drinks."

"Tell you what," she began after she'd walked to the kitchen area. "Why don't you escort Miss Featherstone to the door while I wash these glasses? We can then have a chit-chat after she's left."

My only thought was for Julia, and I didn't hesitate to reach for her hand, which she gladly accepted. We didn't speak until we'd made it out the main door of the building. I took her other hand, and she looked up at me, tears welling in her eyes.

"You must understand, Nathan, it wasn't just a job for me. I genuinely grew to like you, and today..." She took a breath and slightly shook her head. "Well, today I've come to more than like you. And please tell me I'm not wrong, but with you having told me all that stuff upstairs, well... I think you may feel the same way... Do you?" At this point, her tears were in full flow.

I let go of her hands and pulled her into a hug. "You mean more to me than anyone I think I've ever met," I said. "I honestly don't know why, as we hardly know each other. There's just something really special and... I honestly can't put my finger on it. Do you know what I mean?"

I felt her give a little chuckle, followed by a sniffle, and as her tears ran down the side of my neck, I heard her whisper, "I feel the same. I think it's meant to be." She pulled her head back, and with the back of her right hand, she brushed away her tears, smearing her mascara in a single motion.

"That's a good look you've got going on there," I said. She let out a small laugh through her tears. "But hey, listen. You've told me where you're going, so I'll come and find you. This isn't the end, you know!"

Julia pulled back sharply. With a sternness I'd never heard in her voice before, she said, "No, definitely not! On no account must you ever try to find me. Not even for a visit. You must understand that we are only minor players in what is a far bigger game, and the powers that be may not appreciate anyone contradicting their better judgment – there is always a purpose behind their decisions, such as to move me, and it is not for us to question them, it could be dangerous for both of us. That would be extremely dangerous for you! You'll understand why later, but that doesn't mean I can't find you. And I will, Nathan. You'll have to wait—I don't know how long, but I promise I will find you."

She gave me a brief kiss on the lips, pulling away before it could turn serious. "Now, I suggest you don't keep the lady waiting. She's not someone you'd want to upset."

She took a step back, blew me a kiss, and turned to walk to her car, fumbling in her jacket pocket for her keys. After climbing in, she started the engine and began pulling away. She glanced at me one last time, trying to muster a brave little smile that almost seemed to work. I half smiled back. And that was it—Julia was out of my life.

I opened the front door and bounded up the stairs. That woman had some serious explaining to do!

Chapter 8

Well, who knew?

I was already speaking before the flat door had closed. "Okay, tell me why you're really here. I'm not stupid; I know it's not anything to do with police business. In fact, I'm not even sure you are police. I mean, how many coppers can afford to wear shoes that expensive to work?"

My attention was drawn to her shoes as she sat on the sofa, her right leg crossed over her left. She had loosened her right shoe, which dangled from her toes, gently flipping with each movement.

"Okay, you need to chill, Nathan. I know it's been a tough day for you."

"It's Mr. Cartwright to you," I shot back, still fuming and in no mood to relax until I got some sort of explanation. I headed straight to the kitchenette, grabbed my glass, and poured myself another brandy, purposely not offering her one.

"I'm sorry, Nathan," she said in a softer tone, though she made a point of continuing to use my first name. "You're right, of course. I should explain why I'm here. First off, I'm actually in the police force, but I've always had a thing for nice shoes. You can be feminine and have a career, you know; it's not illegal." She flashed me the first smile of the evening.

"But what about Miss Featherstone? Why the hell were you so rude to her? What did she ever do to upset you?"

"Ah, yes, the beautiful Julie." She sighed, her tone dripping with condescension. "You've got quite the thing for her, haven't you, Nathan?" She gave me a playful wink.

I turned away, hoping to hide the blush I felt creeping up my neck, pretending to return the brandy bottle to the cupboard. Then, I went on the offensive.

"My relationship with Julia has absolutely nothing to do with you."

"Your relationship has EVERYTHING to do with me."

I spun around at the venom in her voice.

And there she was, standing inches from my face.

Somehow, she'd slipped her shoe back on, stood, circled the coffee table, and approached me in what must have been a second. Even more unsettling, I hadn't heard a sound or felt her movement at all.

"You see, Nathan, you and I aren't so different." She looked me straight in the eyes as if nothing out of the ordinary had just occurred. "You know, I think I will have a drink after all," she added, having already retrieved the bottle from the cupboard without me even noticing. She poured herself a brandy and returned to the sofa. I stood there, gawking in silence.

"I'm sorry for shouting, but you must understand—people like us have to follow certain rules. Let me explain, and hopefully, the events of the last 24 hours will start to make some sense. And for God's sake, Nathan, just chill. Relax, you look like you've seen a ghost!"

Her smile was disarming, but I was still too stunned to say anything. I replaced words with a submissive nod.

"Okay, let me tell you a bit about myself and where Julia fits into all this. Are you sure you don't want to sit down?" She motioned to the space beside her on the sofa. "This could take a while."

I considered accepting her offer, but still uncertain about who or what I was dealing with, I thought it better to decline.

"I'm actually fine here, thanks. I could use the exercise after sitting in that interview room all day." I forced a small smile, trying to show her that nothing was bothering me, even though it clearly was.

"That's fine," she replied, her smile seeming genuine. "But the offer stands. Now, where was I? Ah, yes, I'm guessing you want to know about me since I know all about you."

Why did this no longer surprise me? Whoever this woman was, she was like no one I'd ever encountered before, and her calm, reassuring demeanor only deepened the mystery surrounding her.

"I'm guessing you've already realized I'm not your everyday type of girl, Nathan. And I'm sorry about the little parlor trick before, but sometimes actions do speak louder than words, and it appears it worked since I've now got your full attention.

"So let me start the beginning. My name is Lucy Donough, spelled D.O.N.O.U.G.H, but I do tend to pronounce it with the first 'o' as a 'u' to make it sound more French. It's actually an American name I picked up over there while living with a family in the 1820s."

That explained her speed. I knew I was fast—very fast for a human, with extremely quick reactions—but that ability improves with age, and she was clearly much older than I. And with age came authority. I returned her smile, hoping it didn't reveal the nervousness I felt inside.

"My role in life is to look after you and your wellbeing. You see, our kind isn't as prevalent as we once were. Wars have taken their toll, and that's why Michael kept you out and away from the World Wars."

So, she knew about Mike and my life at the Fayre!

"I see you're surprised, Nathan," she said with a knowing smile before taking a sip of Brandy. "You know, this is really good. Cheers!"

I responded by unconsciously raising my glass in a return salutation.

"So, you work for someone then?" I asked.

"Oh, yes, but not just anyone; I work for someone rather special, someone you actually know quite well! His name is Lord Gerald Peterson, and he made his fortune on the Stock Market. He's a major shareholder in some of the biggest investment companies in the UK. But that's not his real name. His real name is Cartwright, and yes, he's one of us."

I couldn't hide the shock that registered on my face.

"Yes, Nathan, Lord Peterson is your father. You see, our kind never really abandon their children; we just move and help them through their lives to ensure they get the best care available. However, the bond between parent and child is never really broken. I mean, you must have wondered who's paid your way through life, such as the rent on this hovel." She gestured around the flat with a look of utter repugnance. "It's always been this way, right from the moment he left you."

"Well, if that's true, where did all my inheritance come from? The check I receive every month? Julia said it came from my father's life insurance and will—"

Lucy's laugh cut me off.

"Ah, yes, the wonderful Julia. She really is a gem." Lucy stood and began to pace between the sofa and window with her brandy in one hand, using her other to emphasize the points she was making. "You see, I can't do it all by myself. We do need foot soldiers like Julia.

"You were her first appointment, you know, and she was doing really well. She got you into school using the pretense of your parent's death when you were young. Plus, she got you this…" She waved her arm around like she didn't know what exactly to call it.

"But why her? Wouldn't it have been easier to get someone… I don't know, maybe a little older?"

Lucy approached me, gliding over the stained beige carpet as if she were on ice, and leaned against the worktop beside me before letting out a soft laugh.

"Money, dear boy. Money!" Lucy gave me a playful nudge with her right elbow, careful not to spill her drink. "Where else could a girl like Julia, working for social services, get the kind of money I pay her? And it's not like Daddy's struggling financially." She followed the comment with another wink. "No, she was doing great. But, as you know, Nathan, she was starting to get a little too close."

I snapped my head to the left.

"Oh, come on, Nathan. You don't think I didn't notice the little touchy-feely things going on at the Station! And besides, any doubts I may have had were confirmed when she called me tonight."

"She called YOU? Why? Why would she do that?"

"She was confused." Lucy gently placed her hand on my forearm. "She knew she'd overstepped, and when she told me that you'd explained everything to her… Perhaps she was also afraid of the consequences. Oh, don't worry. It was time for her to move on anyway, and as she probably told you, those arrangements were already in place. I promise you, she will be perfectly safe and we'll continue to look after her. At the end of the day, perhaps it's better if she has an understanding of the world we've introduced her to. But the point is, she can't have any further contact with you. It has to be a clean break, for both of your sakes."

The last part sounded more than a little ominous, but something told me Lucy was telling the truth. I found myself actually warming to her. Normally, someone with her looks and figure might have stirred other emotions in me, but I already viewed her as a kind of surrogate mother, and that felt entirely wrong. Besides, Julia was still fresh in my thoughts—I missed her already.

"I still don't fully see how you fit in," I said, looking into Lucy's eyes that gave absolutely nothing away.

"I'm here to keep an eye on you," she said, staring into her glass. "You've probably never even noticed me, which, if that's the case, means I did a good job! Don't get me wrong, I'm not a stalker. In the past, there were weeks, even months, between my visits, but luckily, I caught you when I did."

"What do you mean, when did you do it? What changed?"

"Pure coincidence. I just happened to pick Friday night to come see you. I was in Wellington when you were there with your mate Billy. You probably didn't notice me because I had my blonde wig on and was with a few of my girlfriends."

Lucy must have seen the surprise on my face because she let out a genuine giggle.

"I do have friends, you know," she said, smiling. "I'm not some gargoyle that appears and disappears in a puff of smoke! I have a life, too. Remember, I'm just a slightly older version of you! Anyway, it should've been a standard night out, and it would've been if I hadn't seen you turn left down Green Street by yourself instead of heading home. I guess I was curious about where you were going. Thankfully, I followed—at a discreet distance. That's when I saw you get into that altercation with those young boys. I mean, what on earth were you thinking?"

"You were there? You saw what happened? Then how come I had to go to the police station? Why couldn't you just say what happened?"

"Oh, come on, Nathan." She shook her head. "Think about what happened. Your stupid actions meant I had to get involved. I didn't want to be, but you left me no option. What would have happened if one of them had gotten in a lucky shot and actually stabbed you, noticing it had absolutely no effect on you? The two of them would have become witnesses to something that would be very difficult to explain. Moreover, you could have put all of our kind in danger... We don't need that kind of publicity!"

She was starting to make sense.

"We can't afford to have witnesses, so I had to step in. I killed the one who tried to stab you but realized the couple who you saved would clearly recognize you. That's why I used the knife to stab you and knock you unconscious.

"Oh, don't look at me like that! I knew the wound would heal, and you'd be fine. And then we had another witness to deal with! That other idiot you thumped looked back over his shoulder while running away and must have seen the whole thing, so I had to handle him too. Well, you know the rest."

Lucy set her drink down, stood directly in front of me, gently grasped my arms, and looked into my eyes.

"You do understand, don't you?" I did, and it all made sense.

"But how did you become a detective investigating the case?" My mind was racing.

Lucy laughed out loud, her shoulders shaking involuntarily.

"I didn't just become one," she said, trying to stifle her laughter. "I've always been one! Think about it: what better job could I have to keep track of what you're doing? I have access to all records—banks, hospitals, social services, you name it—plus evidence. Okay, there's a little paperwork involved, but I suspect you already know how persuasive I can be."

I smiled back, not even realizing I was doing so. Oh, yes, I imagined she could be very persuasive when she needed to be.

"Anyway, after Friday night's little debacle, your father and I have decided it's time for you to move on. You're attracting too much attention. Besides, you're due a school move anyway."

"Swindon would be good," I said with a hopeful smile.

"You know that can't be the case. You need to get Julia out of your head."

Easier said than done! Right at that moment, I'd never needed her more—some sort of stability and a reassuring hug. I decided that was something that I didn't need to tell Lucy.

"In fact, what we've decided is that you should completely move on. And by that, I mean a new life completely. You've already started to outgrow the 17-year-old lifestyle. I mean, Christ, you could probably ace every A-Level exam ever produced the amount of time you've been in there! It won't be long before people start to realize you're not the ordinary sixth former everyone thinks you are. No, we've decided that you need to enter the next phase, so we're moving you to America to start a fresh life."

"America?! Why there? I mean, it's not as if everyone in the UK knows who or what I am. Why not Scotland? Wales?—"

"No, America would be perfect for you. We've found this city an hour south of Atlanta, which is quite nice, but as with many cities, there are areas where it is very rough with quite a lot of shootings. Plus, the Georgian girls are generally, to put it politely, quite a bit larger than here, in the UK. You see, when you get a little bit older, which you will after you arrive, you'll need to feed more. It's just something you'll have to get used to, I'm afraid."

I thought about protesting, but it was clear from Lucy's voice that any form of resistance would be futile. Having seen what she could be like when she was annoyed, I preferred this version.

Lucy fished her car key from her jacket pocket and started to make her way to the door. "Thanks for the Brandy," she said without looking back as she walked away. "A taxi will be here at 0600 Monday morning with your flight tickets, so you've got a day to pack, which should be plenty of time. Have a safe journey, and don't even think about saying your goodbyes. Get in the taxi and go."

She paused with her hand on the door handle and looked at me with a face devoid of emotion.

"And don't even think of doing anything stupid. Remember, someone will be watching you at all times. And although you may think you're special, special doesn't mean indispensable. Bon Voyage, Nathan," she said, offering a smile before leaving my flat.

I walked over to the window to watch her leave the building, but after two minutes, I still didn't see her emerge. I quickly made my way to the flat door, then down to the landing to get a better view of the front door. She was nowhere to be seen. Perhaps this should have surprised me, but after the past 24 hours, I don't think anything would have surprised me anymore.

I returned to my flat and locked the door behind me. Leaning against it, I took in the sight of the place I'd called home for the past few years. For the first time, I felt a pang of sentimentality. But I supposed this was bound to happen sooner or later. Life must go on.

"Well, time to get packing, I suppose."

Chapter 9

Girl Power

Sometimes, your future life is mapped out by your own past experiences, and this is particularly true for Lucy Donough. Born in the Cotswolds in 1658 to farming parents who already had four boys ranging from 3 years to 15 years, it quickly became apparent that she was indeed different from the rest of the children. Of course, her parents knew the reason why and did their best to hide her uniqueness for the first few years, but the natural curiosity of children meant a more drastic solution was needed. And it wasn't just the children. The family's local village was hardly the beautiful biscuit tin picture of the Cotswolds as it is today, but more a hive of resentment amongst barely educated individuals always looking to blame something or somebody for their own ills, and Lucy, despite her very young age, would have been the perfect target.

The solution was to relocate her to new adoptive parents earlier than usual, and where better to get lost in the crowds than a newly thriving London?

As could probably be expected, being torn from her family at such a young age and plunged into a lifestyle she could never have imagined left the young girl very fearful and anxious, which led to her resenting her 'new' parents and blaming them for everything. Ordinarily, her new parents should have recognized this and done their best to reassure her, but this was during an age when if you didn't conform, you were either punished or left to fend for yourself, or worse, both.

Even when dead cats and dogs started to turn up drained of blood, her parents turned a blind eye. Her new father, a watchmaker by trade, did try to make an effort, and for a few years, Lucy's life did start to improve; however, things took a drastic turn for the worse when, in 1665, bodies started to appear in the streets on a regular basis. With an increasing number of unexplained fatalities, her new father and mother became increasingly nervous, particularly when overhearing conversations about witches and curses. A year later, the Great Plague of London had really started to take hold, and Lucy was increasingly left to fend for herself, often finding herself alone on the streets at night. Inherently dangerous during the daytime, the back streets of London were even worse at night, and a young girl was particularly vulnerable, especially now since just one more unexplained death would go largely unnoticed.

It was on one such cold autumnal night that Lucy, as she often did, made her way down the stinking back streets towards one of the local ale houses as there would usually be a fire lit somewhere to provide the locals some warmth, particularly the whores for whom more clothing meant less money. The streets were particularly muddy tonight, and Lucy could feel it squelching between her toes, but at least she had the sense to stick to under the eaves of the houses to prevent being covered in excrement emptied out of the piss pots. She eventually arrived at the Cat and Fiddle, a popular haunt for the Thames dockers and so, by association, a few ladies of the night. Lucy wrapped her tattered shawl tighter around her shoulders and walked over to the ablaze brazier, pleased to see her friend Mary there. Mary was one of the whores who frequented the area, and although of diminutive stature, she wouldn't take any shit from the drunk dockers, and having taken somewhat of a shine to Lucy, she also protected her. And this was necessary since it wasn't unusual for the poorer people to whore out their young daughters to make ends meet.

The warmth of the fire from the brazier and the sound of Mary cursing a fat drunk started to make life a little more bearable, and for the first time in a while, Lucy noticed she was feeling hungry. Thankfully Lucy's kind could go days without food and not feel hungry, but the smell of the gruel emanating from the alehouse and finally overpowering the stench of piss and B.O. had started to make her feel hungry. Lucy closed her eyes while breathing in the smell, only to be awoken by the ringing of a bell. She opened her eyes to see the body collectors in their grotesque masks wheeling their carts piled high with the dead towards the high street. It was then she noticed the man leaning against the corner of the alehouse, smoking a clay pipe and staring at her in a way that made her feel uncomfortable. Unconsciously, she brushed up against Mary for comfort but was met by Mary's hand gently pushing her away; Mary was negotiating a business deal with a young drunk, and the way he was staring at her barely covered and heaving cleavage suggested he wasn't going to get the price he was perhaps hoping for.

Oh, to hell with it. It was time to go back to the house anyway before it got too cold, and the real drunks started to pour out and start fighting. No one ever tried to stop a fight because it was generally accepted that if they weren't knocking ten bells of shit out of each other, then there would be a good chance they would transfer their rage to their poor wives when they got home.

Lucy turned away and headed back the way she had come down the side street of the pub. She had barely got to the ale house's drayman's hatch before she felt the blow to the side of her head and felt a rough hand drag her into the alley, lifting her clean off her feet. The blow had her head ringing, and she could already smell her own blood over the stench of the city, but the feel of the man's other hand roughly forcing its way up the inside of her dress and slamming into her private parts quickly snapped her back to reality. Having no underwear to form a barrier, the pain of his hand trying to enter her spurred Lucy into action, allowing her to take advantage of the position she was in. Being so little, the rapist hadn't felt the need to set her back on the ground but was instead pinning her up against the wall by the top of her dress, causing it to ride up even further. This gave Lucy her chance. With a speed that surprised even her, she abandoned the vane hope of holding the bottom of her dress down and instead brought both hands up together to grab the man's head, and in one swift move, she had latched onto his neck with her mouth with a clamp so fierce that it allowed her to rip open his neck with her free hands. The man tried to scream but could only gargle as he dropped to the floor with blood spurting uncontrollably from his wound.

The blood never tasted so good. It was the first human blood Lucy had tasted, with the exception of her mother's placenta following her birth, and despite knowing it was wrong, she drank until she could stomach no more. She had been told that blood would replenish all her energy, but right now, she had never felt so tired. Perhaps this was how the rich folk felt after they had eaten so much, but Lucy had never experienced that particular luxury. Instead, she crawled behind a few beer barrels awaiting collection, and having seen that the dead man was out of sight of the side street in the shadows, Lucy quickly fell asleep, feeling quite warm for the first time that evening.

Lucy was awoken by a hand shaking her shoulder and immediately tried to go on the offensive, but the strength of the stranger's hand prevented her from moving.

"Still yourself, child, I'm not here to harm you."

Lucy focused her eyes on the well-dressed man who had spoken to her, but her head was buzzing with confusion she didn't understand. The man released his grip and moved his hand down to Lucy's elbow to help her out from behind the barrels. The man spoke again as he gently but firmly eased her out from her seclusion.

"Pray, do not be alarmed, child. I've seen this type of thing before, but I doubt you have – best you take this to cover yourself," and with that, he removed his black cloak lined with red silk and wrapped it around her shoulders.

It was only then that Lucy fully understood what the man was referring to, and the sight that befell her led her to let out a shriek that was instantly quelled by a hand that moved to her mouth so quickly she never even saw it coming. Gone was the small girl; instead, she was looking at the body of a young lady, largely naked due to the torn child's dress.

Before she knew it, she was on her feet with the man lifting her up as if she weighed no more than a bag of flour but with a gentleness that made her instantly warm to him.

"Who are you sir?", asked Lucy, surprising herself with how different and grown up her voice sounded, "my name's Lucy."

"Well, Miss Lucy, my name is Peterson, Gerald Peterson, and if you don't mind me saying so, I could also be your lord and savior! But take no heed of an old man's ramblings. Right now, I'm sure you would benefit more from a hot bath, some more befitting clothes, and a good meal, and by that, I don't mean the kind of fayre you partook of last night," and with that, he nodded over at the drunk's prone body, now barely recognizable as a human being. "And do not worry yourself about that unfortunate soul; it won't be the first time the local constabulary find a drunk killed outside such an establishment."

Peterson smiled down reassuringly at Lucy, the look of shock and realization still etched on her face. He reached down and clasped her hand and with his other hand clad in a soft white silk glove gently turned her chin away from the scene.

"Let's go to your new home, shall we?" He suddenly halted in his tracks and looked directly at Lucy. "I mean, if that's satisfactory to you, my dear. I'm of the mind that should you suddenly appear back at your own house looking like", and taking a moment to collect his thoughts while gesturing at her with his spare hand, continued, "Well, looking resoundingly different to when you left."

Lucy didn't quite know what to say, so didn't but instead looked up at the handsome man and tried to smile at him while also aware that a tear was running down her cheek. And with that, her new master led her gently out of the smog into what was about to become a sunny but cold day.

It turned out that Peterson's house was only a few streets away but, in an area, totally unfamiliar to Lucy. It wasn't healthy for poor people to venture into the rich suburbs of London unless they worked there, and even then, if you didn't have an excuse off-pat for the local constabulary, you could still find yourself walking the treadmill for a few days in the local jail.

The house was like nothing Lucy could have imagined. A three-story terraced mews house, Lucy could barely bend her neck back enough to see the rooftop when stood on the steps. The imposing black front door opened as if by magic, and Lucy was led slowly inside.

"Thank you, Lizzie", said Peterson while handing her his bowler hat and gloves to a beautiful blond lady dressed in a striking red floor-length dress pulled in by a corset at the waist emphasizing a very matronly bosom. "This is Miss Lucy whom I came upon this morn and, as you can probably observe, is a little worse for wear. If you don't mind, I'll hand you my cloak once Miss Lucy has been provided with more, shall we say, fitting garments. However, right now, I think a hot bath would be in order, so I'd be obliged if you could do me the honor."

Peterson then turned to look directly at Lucy and taking both her hands in his noticed that she was shaking slightly. It couldn't have been the house since it was more than warm with having the fires lit first thing.

"I realize all this must come as quite shocking, Lucy, but again, I assure you that you'll be perfectly safe here. The front door is always unlocked, and you're free to leave at any time. However, I suggest that you get yourself cleaned up first and have a nice hot meal inside you before you make any rash decision. Miss Elizabeth here will look after you and provide you with everything you need, and I'll check up on you once you look a little bit more presentable." And with that, Gerald Peterson gave Lucy a warm, reassuring smile that would stay with her for the rest of her life.

No sooner had he finished speaking than he let go of Lucy's hand, only for it to be replaced with a warm, smaller hand. Lucy turned to look at Miss Elizabeth, who was smiling back at her.

"Please call me Lizzie, my dear; Master Peterson does like his formalities, but we ladies need to stick together! And don't worry, I won't bite", which caused both Peterson and Lizzie to look at each other with an amused smirk. "Come on then, let's get that bath ready."

Once they had climbed the stairs, and not one flight but two, Lucy really did feel like she had died and gone to heaven. She couldn't get over the opulence of the building; everything was so clean with ornaments that a few times caused Lucy to stop in her tracks only to be pulled on by Lizzie.

"You'll get used to all this over time, my dear", she said, stopping and turning to Lucy with a worried look on her face. "Assuming you do decide to stay that is!" she continued.

Lizzie didn't wait for the answer. She was confident Lucy would come and instead let out a little laugh, saying, "Of course, you'll stay. Now, here we are, why don't you go over to that dressing room over there and pick out something to wear? I'd stick to something loose and easy to get into for now; tomorrow, we can go shopping for some proper clothes! Now, once you've found something, head through that door there, and it will take you through to the bathroom; I'll meet you there. The bath won't take long as we always have water on the fire." With that, Lizzie left Lucy to go hunting for something to wear.

Lucy eventually picked a white robe buttoned up the front, which she assumed was some form of sleepwear; it was clear that these rich folk didn't sleep in the one set of clothes they owned.

Arriving in the bathroom, Lizzie knelt, stirring the hot water in the tub and occasionally topping it up with more hot water to get the temperature just right. Lucy said nothing but watched Lizzie with enquiring eyes. Although she was probably doing the chores of a maid, her dress was beautiful, and the coal over her eyes and delicately applied rouge to her cheeks and lips suggested she was anything but a maid. This wasn't the makeup Lucy was used to seeing on the whores —thick and garish. Lizzie's makeup was so subtle, enhancing her natural beauty. She truly was stunning.

Lizzie must have read Lucy's thoughts because she surprised Lucy with her opening piece of conversation.

"It's not what you think my dear. There is nothing untoward going on between the master and I, we are just good friends I assure you", and with that, she gave Lucy a little wink.

Lucy immediately felt herself blush violently. "I didn't think for one minute", before stopping mid-sentence aware that she had no idea what she was going with this, and also still being surprised at the sound of her new voice.

This caused Lizzie to let out a bellowing but ladylike laugh, clearly amused at Lucy's embarrassment. "You come over here," beckoning to the steaming tub, "and get yourself all relaxed. Please spend as much time as you like there; there's no urgency, and I'll go downstairs and get some hot food ready for you. When you've finished – the towels are on the seat by the bath – please feel free to join us downstairs, right down to the bottom of the stairs, and the drawing room is on your right."

Lizzie turned to face away from Lucy and held out her right hand, unsure whether Lucy would know her left from her right. As it transpired, Lucy did know her left from her right but didn't have a clue what the hell a 'druwin room' was.

Lucy had never experienced luxury like the bath before, and after using the soap that was so fragrant it made her senses tingle, she fell asleep breathing in the warm steam. This truly was heaven, and she never wanted to wake up from the dream. Eventually, of course, the water started to cool, and it was the drop in temperature that awoke her. Stepping out of the bath, she used the fluffiest towel she had ever felt to start drying herself off. The knock on the door signified that Lizzie must have come back to see what was taking her so long.

"Come in," shouted Lucy, dropping her towel to pick up her robe.

"I do beg you pardon," exclaimed the deep voice behind her, "I thought you would already be dressed for lunch; I, I didn't mean; I really do apologize."

Lucy turned around quickly holding her robe up in front to protect her modesty to be confronted by Peterson who now had his back turned to her with his hand still across his eyes.

This caused Lucy to laugh saying, "You can take your hand down sir, the free show is over! Are you telling me you don't like what

70

you say, I mean I'm growing to really like it myself!"

Lucy thought her remark was quite quirky, so she was surprised by the anger she was met with.

"Get dressed and we'll continue with this conversation downstairs". And then in a calmer voice, Peterson again apologized before leaving the bathroom and closing the door behind him.

Lucy entered the drawing room like a schoolgirl waiting to be chastised by the headmaster. However, her fear was somewhat unfounded as it was Mater Peterson who made the first apology. "I'm so sorry for bursting in like that, I never thought. Well, you know, I am genuinely sorry."

Lizzie continued to thaw the conversation by adding, "It's perfectly understandable, my dear; the Master is not used to having two women around the house; I think I'm already more than he can cope with. Listen, I know you two have got quite a lot to talk about so I'll leave you to it while I serve up lunch next door." And with that, Lizzie walked over and affectionately kissed Peterson on the forehead before leaving the room, closing the double doors behind her.

Lucy felt compelled to speak first.

"I'm so sorry, sir, but in my life, when you have no money, the easiest way to say thank you to someone you are truly grateful to is to offer them the use of your body. I just thought you may have found me attractive."

"And in any other life, I may have taken you up on the offer, my dear. God did indeed bestow on you a beauty rarely seen, and one day, I'm sure you'll learn how to exploit that beauty, but not how you may think. However, as beautiful as you are, the first thing that attracted me to you was finding you in dire need of help and knowing that you are one of our kind."

71

The look of surprise on Lucy's face caused him to stop in his tracks.

"Oh yes," he continued, I am like you also, but obviously far older. I've seen and experienced things you've never dreamed of, and I only ask that you never question me about my past, as I don't want it to influence how you'll live your long life.

"Now, I never got to say what the final thing was that made me so attracted to you, and that is because you remind me so much of my daughter. And before you enquire as to her whereabouts, it pains me to tell you she died many years ago in a period known as the Spanish Inquisition. This was when the catholic church tortured and killed anyone slightly different, and we, my dear, certainly fall into that category. Well, my daughter, Isobell, unfortunately, got captured by the inquisitors and couldn't escape without causing harm to other innocents. Her problems really began when the torture started. It wasn't any confession through the torture that got her killed; it was the speed at which her wounds healed that attracted all the attention, something she, unfortunately, could do nothing about. She did try to use her speed to escape, but by a cruel twist of fate, she slipped in her own blood, fracturing her ankle. So, from then on, they broke the same ankle at the beginning of each day. It doesn't matter how fast you are if you can only run in circles!"

Lucy could see his attempt at humor was only made to hide the clear pain that crossed his face. She could see his eyes welling up with tears, which caused Lucy to also start crying.

"Anyway", Peterson continued after clearing the lump from his throat, "she ended up taking her own life by smashing her head against the cell wall. A very brave girl. And that, my dear, is what I see in you, a brave young girl with a difficult start in life. However, with the right guidance that I believe I can provide you, I would like nothing else but for you to live the life my daughter should have had. Of course, I will look after you through it all, albeit sometimes from a distance, but know this. I will love you like my own daughter."

Again, Lucy had no idea how to respond and didn't. She was still choked up over the death of Isobelle.

Peterson had composed himself far faster than Lucy. Looking directly at her from his deep seat by the roaring fire, he looked at Lucy deep in her eyes as if penetrating her very soul.

"Our first task will be to integrate you into today's high society."

Lucy gave him a puzzled look.

"Integrate, Sir?"

Peterson laughed at her genuinely puzzled expression.

"And that, my dear girl, is why we need to whisk you off to France away from all this pestilence, squalor, and shit. You see, Miss Elizabeth and I go a long way back. She, too, is one of our kind from a very distinguished family with the name Donough. She made what may be described as 'an unfortunate error of judgment' back in Paris – it's the capital of France Lucy," noticing Lucy's look of puzzlement again. "Anyway, she had to flee overseas, so she joined me here as my maid. When I say 'maid,' she clearly isn't, but while everyone in high society needs to know everything about anyone who matters, no one will ever question where a maid came from! We've been discussing her return to France for some years now, and now here you are, you've made the decision for us! And she also has a beautiful daughter there called Celine who looks about your age, but actually is in her teens and I'm sure you'll bond perfectly. You will, of course, have to remain largely anonymous for the first few years, as we all had to, in order to allow your brain's growth to catch up with your physical transformation. That's if you don't mind, of course; Lizzie's already told me she thinks you're absolutely adorable."

Lucy raised herself from the sofa and walked across to Peterson, and emulating Lizzie's earlier departure, gently kissed Peterson's forehead. "I'd like nothing better Sir and will forever be in your debt."

That bond that formed between them became very tight over the years that followed. Gerald treated her with the utmost respect, and over the next few years, Lucy became the original Eliza Doolittle, transforming from a neglected street urchin into a beautiful young lady seamlessly blending into high society away from the rats and the unfortunate.

As with most things in life, nothing comes for free, but Lucy would have done anything for the man she loved, but she knew she could never love like she so wanted to. There were no secrets between the two of them, and Gerald had taught her everything about surviving in a world that had never understood their like. There was no doubt that Lucy wouldn't have survived had it not been for Gerald's intervention, and she took every opportunity to remind him of the fact. And it was this that went on to shape her future life, as both she and her beloved mentor realized that future generations could probably benefit from someone assigned to look after them too, and who better to carry out the vetting process than someone who had already benefited from the same help. And so, it was to be that Lucy would become a headhunter for future keepers.

Many years later, Lucy came across Julia on her search for potential keepers. Lucy was immediately attracted to Julia as they had so much in common. Julia wasn't one of their kind, but past experience had proven that having someone with blood thirst looking after another would often lead to clashes of egos, which could soon turn messy. Not too much of an issue for Lucy, who, despite maintaining a

74

very lady-like demeanor, could switch back to that urchin-in-survival mode at the flick of a switch, and that certainly wasn't a pretty sight to behold. But no, Julia was perfect.

Coming from a broken home with both her parents dependent on crack, Julia quickly learned to become an independent young woman while living in various foster homes. However, all the moving around meant Julia never had any real friends, so when one evening this beautiful young lady in the pub introduced herself as Lucy and took her dancing, for the first time she really felt for who she was, not dismissed offhand simply because of where she had come from. And then came the job offer Lucy found in social services, something she would have never dreamed of without having a degree.

Julia found her new job a little challenging at first, but Lucy was always on hand to provide advice and guidance; perhaps because Lucy was a police officer, she got to work with social services a lot.

"So, you're still loving the job then?" asked Lucy while gently sipping her glass of Pino.

Julia was, as usual, staring in admiration at Lucy's high heels.

"I still don't know how you can wear heels that long for work, still you certainly have the legs for them," and with that, Julia clinked her own glass of Pino against her friend's.

"Yeah, the job's good, and it pays the rent. I really can't thank you enough, Luce."

Julia really *couldn't* thank her enough. Of course, the money was great, which did seem a little high for a public servant, but no one ever questions a high salary! It also seemed strange that one of her clients, Nathan Cartwright, seemed to have a wealthy benefactor yet lived in a bedsit! However, one of the rules in social services is that you don't divulge or discuss anything about your clients as it is strictly confidential, and anyway, to be fair, Julia did find him quite quirky and cute!

"Well, what would you think if I told you I could probably get you another job that got you your own house – all paid for and in your name – plus a very generous salary?"

Julia laughed but stopped abruptly, noticing that Luce wasn't joining in the laughter.

"OMG, you're serious, aren't you? So, what's the catch, Luce? What does it involve?" The excitement and confusion were written equally across Julia's face; she was like a diabetic in a bakers.

Lucy grabbed Julia's hand and, with her other hand, took Julia's glass of Pino out of her hand and placed it on the table.

"Hey girl, if you think I'm discussing work on our Friday night out together, you're sadly mistaken! I'll call you later, and everything will be clear. Now, let's go dance before that dude's eyes at the bar crawl even further up those gorgeous legs you've been tottering around on." And with that, both walked briskly to the dance floor, treating the guy at the bar to that 'thanks, but no thanks' look while at the same time making sure they displayed as much leg as possible.

Their regular Friday nights were always good for both girls, and they were super close and had no secrets. So, it did come as some surprise to Julia a few weeks later when Lucy called her up just before she was due to accompany Nathan to the police station for an interview. Lucy requested Julia pretend not to recognize her during the interview as it would 'be in Nathan's best interest.' It definitely seemed strange, but hell, Julia liked both of them, and she trusted her Luce implicitly.

Chapter 10

Welcome to the Land of the Free

Stood at the bottom of the steps leading up to the flats, I saw the car arrive at 0600 on the dot. I could see the driver looking for a space to park, but as usual that bloody Transit van was taking up what was two spaces. Seemingly unperturbed by the two cars behind him, the driver got out, opened the rear door and boot and beckoned me over with just the words "Mr Cartwright."

I walked to the car, tossed my two small bags into the boot, and glanced at the driver stuck behind us, offering a silent apology for the delay. He responded with a casual raise of his hand on the steering wheel and a slight nod—hardly surprising, given that my driver was a cool-looking, built like a brick-shithouse black guy. I didn't want to add to the waiting driver's delay, so I jumped into the back seat. Before I had time to fasten my seatbelt, the car was already in motion.

My obligatory British greeting of "Morning" was met with dead silence. After a long enough pause to make it clear he wasn't to be disturbed, my driver spoke in a voice so deep it suggested his build wasn't entirely due to gym sessions. He informed me that there was a manila envelope in the seat pocket and that I should open it and read its contents.

The letter inside the envelope was brief, to say the least. It simply read, *"Everything you'll need is in here. Take care of it. You will be met at Atlanta Airport by a lady called Lizzie Simmons."* That was it—no signature, nothing.

I tipped the contents out onto the back seat and began sorting through them. Whoever had put this together certainly knew what they were doing. Inside the package was a passport with a work permit visa, bank cards, a medical insurance card, even a Social Security card, and $1000 in various denominations. There were also details of my flight, which, to my surprise, was first class.

Instead of feeling relieved, especially about the cash—I'd been worried about how I was going to pay for the 'taxi' since I woke up—I felt more perplexed. This wasn't a regular taxi, that much was clear. My first thought was: how had they managed all of this in such a short time? How had they gotten everything without me having to sign anything? I'd never even visited a Chase Bank, either in person or online.

With one question opening up more difficult ones, I decided to push it all aside. Perhaps it was just a perk of having a Peer of the Realm for a father, which caused me to smile a little.

Without so much as a "safe travels" from the driver, I was unceremoniously dropped outside Heathrow Terminal 3 with my two small bags before he sped off. After checking in, I managed to find a café—one of those places that charge restaurant prices—that actually cooked steaks to order. I satisfied my hunger with a rare steak and plenty of greens, washed down with beetroot juice I'd picked up at one of those "everything you'll ever need for your flight" shops.

It's funny to think that if only the health food junkies who introduced these juice products knew, they'd be partly responsible for me not using them for their intended purpose!

The flight itself was incredibly comfortable, with most of it spent sleeping in my first-class bed after indulging in a cheeky red wine or two—definitely the way to travel. Upon arrival in Atlanta, passport control wasn't too bad. After explaining that my "work" would be casual bar work to earn some money over the summer, they seemed fairly nonchalant. Perhaps it was the fact that I looked like a teenager and was unaccompanied, making me hardly seem like a threat to national security.

Once I picked up my two small bags, the sum of all my personal belongings, I entered the arrivals terminal, scanning the crowd for Lizzie, who was supposed to meet me. There were about 20 to 30 people there greeting new arrivals. As I walked down the area between the exit barriers, I quickly scanned the crowd and noticed two unaccompanied women, each holding a sign—neither of which had my name on it. Fantastic. Just what I needed. I was about to turn around and retrace my steps when I heard a voice behind me.

Turning around, I found myself face-to-face with a skinny guy, probably in his late 20s. He was dressed in jeans and a green collared shirt, topped off with a sports jacket—smart but casual, the kind of look that said he'd put just enough thought into his appearance without trying too hard. His smile was genuine, almost disarming, but what really caught my attention were his blue eyes and shoulder-length brown hair swept back effortlessly. Definitely a ladies' man, and I got the distinct impression he knew I knew.

"I'm sorry to disappoint you," he said, his tone light. "I know you were expecting Lizzie, but she's been reassigned, so I guess you're stuck with me! I'm Mason. Mason Green. I'll be looking after you until you get settled."

With that, Mason extended his hand, and I dropped my bag to shake it. His grip was firm, the kind you'd expect from someone who was comfortable and in control—a confident young man.

"Hey, let's get you to your new home as you must be tired from such a long flight. Can I help you with the bags?" He said this while glancing down at my two pathetic little bags and saved my embarrassment by already turning to walk away before I had a chance to respond.

"Do you need anything to eat and drink before we set off; it's only about an hour to get there depending on the traffic?". I thanked Mason and told him I'd rather just go straight home to which Mason responded with "Gotcha buddy, and you can get some sleep in the car."

I didn't need any encouragement to sleep. As soon as we hit the I-75, I dozed off, only waking when we arrived at the house. And what a house it was—definitely a step up from my old bedsit. From the outside, it appeared to be a spacious bungalow, but it wasn't until we stepped inside that I truly appreciated its size. The entrance hall alone was bigger than my entire flat, and it led into a bright, airy sitting room with tasteful furniture and a 78-inch flatscreen TV that fit seamlessly into the space.

Mason showed me to my double bedroom, one of four equally sized rooms, with a king-sized bed positioned facing the door. He told me to drop my bags, promising a quick tour of the house afterward.

"Are you too tired for a drink?" asked Mason while reaching into the fridge for a cold Miller Lite, "I have quite a selection – it doesn't have to be a beer."

"A beer's fine, planes always make you so dehydrated. But just one, please, as more than anything, I'd just like to shower off the journey and climb into that massive bed! What time do I have to be up tomorrow? I mean I don't even know what I'm supposed to be doing for work."

Mason flopped onto a couch large enough to seat a family of six and let out a hearty laugh in response to my question. "Oh, don't worry about work. You won't be doing anything for the next few days except settling in—work comes later. Sleep as long as you like tomorrow; I've got a few errands to run. There's plenty of food in the kitchen and tons of channels on the TV, though 99% of them are garbage, so just keep yourself entertained. I should be back around 6 p.m., and then we'll go out. I'll show you some real Southern hospitality."

Chapter 11

Moonshine and Shadows

T rue to his word, at about 6 p.m., I heard the front door open from my kitchen seat. In walked Mason, carrying two bags of shopping, which he placed on the kitchen island where I was sitting drinking what is laughingly classed as tea over here. Mason glanced down at my drink and let out a suppressed laugh.

"See, I was thinking of you, Nathan. I've got you something that should make you feel a little more at home." Rummaging to the bottom of the first bag produced a box of Tetley's Breakfast Tea.

"You've probably guessed by now that we rarely drink hot tea over here – you only need to look at the damn weather forecast to understand why – what you're drinking there is what we make iced sweet tea from!"

I smiled and thanked him, feeling it wouldn't appear too rude to get up, tip the American tea down the sink, and fill the kettle.

"Fancy a proper cup?" I asked over my shoulder, to which he replied, "Thank you kindly, sir, but I'm fixing to get my liquid intake tonight!"

His accent just reminded me of the film Deliverance; it was so slow and methodical. I realized that in order to try and adopt the accent, all you have to do is take the first vowel of the word you're saying and then add three more of the same vowels, so 'Nathan' is pronounced 'Naaaathan'. And there you have it: you're one step away from learning the banjo!

"I remembered after I left this morning that all the meat we have is frozen, so I took the liberty of getting a couple of steaks for us to eat before we go out; do you mind me cooking?"

The steaks he was referring to were about 1½" thick Ribeye steaks, and it only dawned on me then how hungry I was – looking at them, I could have eaten one raw.

"Of course not," I replied, conscious that the more polite I tried to sound, the more English I sounded.

It was as if he read my mind as he responded with "You sure do have a classy accent, my friend, the ladies will be throwing themselves at you tonight if they hear you speak! Go and watch some TV and I'll holler when supper is ready."

I decided to do just that, so I thanked Mason and sat down to watch the huge TV. I wasn't really focused on what was on for two reasons. The first was because I'd tried to watch a film earlier in the afternoon and realized that the closer you got to the end, the more frequent and longer the advertisements were. And to make it worse, every advert seemed to be a medical one trying to convince fat people that they didn't need to diet, just take this pill, and they'll do all these jolly activities for the rest of their lives. I mean, how can that be even legal? But my second reason was more legitimate. I was having trouble feeling at ease with Mason and never really knew what to say to him. Don't get me wrong, he was as friendly as can be and was nothing but nice to me, but my head was swimming with questions such as why am I here, what the 'work' I would be doing, and how did he seem to know so much about me? He just didn't seem to want to open up, but maybe he was a little nervous, having never met me before.

The sound and smell of the steaks hitting the hot cast iron

pans snapped me out of my thoughts, and I found myself staring at yet another bloody medical advert. I was going to go back into the kitchen before realizing that it would mean me having to indulge in further small talk so I settled down to watch more Type 2 diabetics skipping around the screen while I listened to all the side effects being listed, which made me think I'd rather take my chance as a diabetic.

It wasn't more than ten minutes later when Mason shouted, "Supper's ready," and I made my way into the kitchen to sit opposite him on the island.

"I'm assuming you wanted yours rare, and I promise the broccoli and green beans are fresh, although I did cheat with the instant mash!" However, I was looking at the steak, which looked delicious and even more so when I cut into it with a knife so big it would have been classed as a weapon of mass destruction in the UK. The steak had been rested for just the right amount of time and was so tender and juicy.

Mason could see my look of admiration, so just said, "Well, eat up; we need to leave at eight. You've probably noticed already that your closet in your bedroom has already been stocked with new clothes that should fit you, so choose what you want to wear tonight – nothing too classy – and remember it will be muggy outside! Welcome to Georgia heat!"

I had noticed the clothes but never thought for one minute they might be mine.

"Hey, there was no need" I began, but was cut off by "nonsense, you're now the head of the household, this house is yours now. Remember, I'm only here to make sure you settle in okay but will then back off – I'm your U.S. version of Julia, but probably not so hot looking, eh?" while giving me a knowing wink.

I shouldn't have been surprised, although I'm sure my expression confirmed otherwise. It may go some way to explain the contents of the envelope I'd been given by the driver on the way to Heathrow. For some reason, I started to immediately feel a little more relaxed and held up my glass of half-decent red wine, offering Mason a hearty "cheers," to which he responded with a "cheers" of his own, although in an attempted 'English' accent. I mean, how can you bugger up just one word? I think he must have been thinking the same thing, as it caused us to both laugh together. Maybe I'd been overthinking the whole situation, perhaps jet lag?

I ended up opting for a long-sleeved white cotton shirt, which fitted perfectly and seemed to go well with the stone-washed jeans. Okay, I still looked a bit pale compared to everyone else out here, but hopefully, that would add to my English charm. Embarrassingly, Mason decided to enter the bedroom following a knock that he must have given while opening the door to find me standing in front of the full-length mirror, smiling at myself.

"Uber will be here in about 5 minutes – are you okay for money, by the way?"

"Yeah, no problem, mate," I replied while maintaining my look in the mirror in an effort to quell further embarrassment. Once the door closed again, I went to the bedside drawer where I'd stashed the dollars I'd been given and placed 100 and two 50 notes in my wallet, which I hoped would be sufficient. A final splash of unidentifiable but clearly expensive aftershave and I heard the front doorbell ring. I treated myself to another quick glance in the mirror before exiting the bedroom and was happy with the man who glanced back at me – looking good, kid!

The Uber pulled off the road into a gravel parking lot in front of what I could best describe as a huge single-story barn made out of wood and metal – certainly not the kind of pub I was used to, but the number of cars trucks and Harleys parked there suggested the place may be buzzing inside.

I wasn't wrong; the place was probably 75% full, and I was met by a cacophony of balls being played on probably eight pool tables, mostly by young men, and with the occasional gaggle of cute girls watching them. Only the conversation from the spacious bar area was louder, briefly interrupted by a 3-piece rock group doing their sound check. The clientele seemed to be mostly in their 30s and dressed very casually, with a few of the younger girls barely dressed at all but exuding that air of confidence you can only get away with when you know you look good and know other people are secretly thinking the same. I already liked the place!

I was aware of my arm being gripped by Mason, who started leading me to the bar. He was clearly a regular here and seemed to be a bit of a favorite with the ladies, many of whom received a fleeting peck on the cheek or a gentle slap on the arse as he made his way through the crowd towards a young lady who was seated at the corner of the bar. Wearing a vest top that served to accentuate the many tattoos on her arms and which just about concealed her boobs, she looked up and smiled at Mason as he approached her.

"Kylie, I'd like to introduce my buddy from England. I'm sure he'll end up being quite a regular here!" Then, looking at me, "Nathan, meet Kylie; she runs the place as manager." I immediately went to shake Kylie's hand, but she used the same hand to pull herself up off her barstool before planting a kiss on my cheek.

"Well, hi Nathan, let me introduce you to some of our people," and with that, she pulled me over to a table and started to introduce me to two young ladies who were obviously regulars. I only said two words, 'Hello ladies', but that was enough for the blonder of the two to respond with, "Why, I love your accent. Are you really English?" And that was that. Within minutes there were six people sitting around the table, all wanting a piece of me and being ever so nice. Mason turned up with a tray filled with four bottles of American beer and six glasses of yellow liquid. The 'yellow' turned out to be a banana liqueur mixed with moonshine, which was a fantastic tasting shot.

As the evening wore on, it became clear that Madeline, a cute little blonde wearing a black leather corset paired with some 'Daisy Duke' denim shorts and cowgirl boots, all of which showed off her toned and tanned figure, was becoming increasingly flirtatious with me. In a way, she kind of reminded me a little of Julia, although slightly less well-endowed on the top, and the way she leaned into me and gazed into my eyes when I was talking did make me feel nice and relaxed. The drinks were also helping! I never even had a chance to buy a round; the Banana shots just kept reappearing as if by magic. It's a good thing Madeline and her friends were great company since, for most of the evening, Mason was off doing his own thing, only returning occasionally with another tray of free drinks. He was certainly a bit of a celebrity at the bar and was maybe just trying to assert his dominance as top dog, but I didn't really care. I again tried to get up to go to the bar and get around in, but the next tray of drinks arrived before I had a chance to stand. We all did the English 'cheers' before downing the shots together, and it was at this point that Medeline placed her hand on the inside of my thigh. I should have brushed it off, but I didn't. This was a really great bar – far better than any I'd ever visited in England.

Chapter 12

Wakey, Wakey, Eggs and Bakey

It was the smell that woke me up. Well, that and the damp patch in the bed. Oh, please don't say I pissed myself! I knew I felt bad and couldn't even remember leaving the bar last night. I tried opening my eyes, but the sun was already lighting up the bedroom through the windows, and the curtains were still open from yesterday, causing me to wince at the light. Knowing now what to expect, I opened them more slowly and tried to ignore the pounding hangover. The sight that met me jolted me wide awake, causing me to try and sit up, only to be prevented from doing so by my left hand being handcuffed to the headboard.

I was instantly wide awake, surveying what could only be described as a horror scene. I managed to suppress the instant wave of nausea that hit me either through the drink, the sight on which I was transfixed, or both. The amount of fresh blood on the bed was now overpowering my senses, causing an instant flashback to when, as a child, I found that poor woman at the fayre, but any chance of satisfying my thirst was thwarted by the handcuffs.

There was no chance of this being classed as an accidental death; the kitchen knife protruding from the poor girl's stomach left nothing to the imagination. She was completely naked and laid on her back with her head tilted away from me. Even though I couldn't see her face due to her matted and blood-soaked hair covering most of it, I knew from the perfume it was Madeline from last night. Or at least what remained of her because it was obvious the knife in her stomach hadn't just been used the once. I prayed that she had died before the other wounds had been inflicted otherwise her pain and suffering must have been unbearable. And it was that thought that tipped the scales, causing me to heave up everything I'd drank last night, with most of it spraying on the poor girl due to my failed attempt at covering my mouth with my free right hand. The reflexing for the second bout had already started as the bedroom door opened, so while I caught sight of Mason entering, I was prevented from saying anything until the second bout, along with the dry coughing that always followed, subsided.

"What the hell have you done?" I shouted in a venomous tone that even surprised me.

No effect on Mason whatsoever. He merely fashioned a look of mock surprise on his face before relaxing into a half smile.

"Well mornin' to you too, sir! Gonna be a mighty fine day," gesturing at the sun now bathing half the room in its light, "someone doesn't sound so happy!"

In order to try and look more authoritative, I used my right sleeve to wipe my mouth and my nose, which I knew was full of sick snot, but buggered if I was going to ask that bastard for a tissue. I decided to try a different approach and took a silent, deep breath before speaking.

"Oh, come on, Mason," I said smiling, "I was just shocked, that's all; what's with the handcuffs? Was she into the kinky stuff? Can you take them off, please, as they're starting to cut in now I'm awake?" Playing dumb may be my best option.

It wasn't.

Mason threw his head back and laughed while simultaneously clapping his hands in glee.

"Sir, you know I can't do that, at least not just yet! Remember, I do know what you are and that you could kill me before I knew what was happening, and that, my friend, wouldn't be good for either of us! No, you see, they stay on, at least until we've had a chance to talk.

Mason pulled up a seat near the left side of my bed, making sure he was just out of reach should I choose to lunge at him. My immediate thought was why he chose that side of the bed; perhaps the sight of the poor girl would put him off his train of thought. He folded his arms across his knees, leaned forward, and continued where he'd left off.

"No, you see the cuffs are for our protection. I'm sure you've got a thousand and one questions, so let me oblige you by telling you what happened last night and that way you may calm down a little."

Mason leaned back in his chair and crossed his legs, so I assumed he would be going into some depth.

"I've got to be honest with you, sir, last night's festivities were kinda planned. Don't get me wrong," he said, raising his hands in a submissive gesture, "All the people there, including the staff and band, were genuine and knew nothing about what was going to happen later. I do know you seemed to be having a great time and you were certainly throwing the drinks back, but we know how you Brits like to drink!"

"But so were you!" And as soon as the words had left my mouth, I was inwardly chastising myself for being so stupid.

Mason knew that I knew but decided to confirm it anyway.

"Ah, the light finally dawns; thank ya, Jesus!" Mason proclaimed, looking up and raising both hands to the ceiling. "You see, those banana shots we were all drinking, well, mine were made with lemonade; the girls were drinking theirs with over-the-counter moonshine, but you, my friend…" He was now shaking his head in mock disbelief, "Yes, you, my friend, you were drinking the shots made with full-blooded redneck moonshine – positively lethal stuff even for us locals! By the time we left, you could hardly stand and had really no idea where you were or what you were doing! Of course, we had to make sure you didn't start to recover, so when we got you into the car, my good friend Joseph administered a little sedative – just to help you sleep, you understand! Oh, I forgot to mention Joseph! You see, when I mention 'we,' I'm talking about Joseph and me – we're childhood friends.

"Once you were nice and sleepy, I went back in to ask Madeline if she wanted a lift home, which isn't unusual since we quite often drop her off at home, so she gratefully accepted and joined us for the ride!"

I noticed that when he said Madeline's name, he couldn't even look at her on the bed.

"But surely someone will miss her and remember her walking out with you," I said, thinking out loud.

"Ah, you're in the good ol' US of A now, my friend! You see, Madeline lives alone in a trailer park and generally keeps to herself. Quite often, she drove up to Tennessee to see her Mother and was due to go on Tuesday, so no one should miss her for at least a few weeks. By then, she would have completely disappeared from the face of the earth with no traces left. Unless, of course, you decide to be a hero, and we're forced to provide the authorities with the photographs we took of the pair of you last night. Which, I must add, are rather quite raunchy, to say the least, and I particularly liked the one of her sitting naked on your lap with you holding the knife to her throat. Oh, and before you ask, she was already dead before, well, all that," he said, waving the back of his hand towards her lifeless corpse but still refusing to look directly at her. She felt no pain at all, and the shot Joseph gave her won't show up should there be any autopsy, but again, the 'autopsy' will depend on your cooperation. Agree to our terms, and everything gets cleaned up, and she disappears. Of course, we will keep the photos for insurance purposes; we're not totally stupid!"

"I will tell you now, Nathan, that the photos have already been sent to multiple people within our organization, and even I have no idea who they are or where they are, so should you agree to listen further to what I have to say and I release your cuffs, killing me will serve you no purpose. If they fail to hear from me regularly, they will come for you, and I don't think you really realize how powerful some of these people are. Now, sir, are you going to play nice?"

Aside from the fact that the cuffs were really starting to be painful, I just needed to distance myself from Madeline, as the smell of blood was making me feel ravenous.

"Okay, you have my word as an Englishman and gentleman, I won't hurt you. That doesn't mean that one day I won't come for you, but with the insurance you claim you have, that won't be soon."

Mason stood up and very cautiously took a step towards the bed, aware now that he was within my reach. Reaching into the pocket of his tailored shorts, he took out the keys, unlocked the cuffs and then, perhaps unconsciously, immediately stepped back and sat back down, as it doing that would make him safer.

As soon as the cuffs were off, I casually swung my legs over the edge of the bed and stood up, resulting in two things at once. Firstly, the pounding of my hangover from standing up too quickly, and secondly, the realization I was completely naked with my meat and two vegs less than a foot away from my captor's face. Ordinarily, that may have amused me, but my priority was to get a huge drink of water and put on a dressing gown.

I was met coming out of the bathroom by Mason, who marshaled me toward the bedroom door. "I think we would both be more comfortable talking in the kitchen, Nathan, don't you? Besides, you look like you could really eat a big breakfast. I'm fixing to fry off some sausages and eggs; does that sound good?"

I nodded my head and sat down at the breakfast bar. I really was hungry and was so glad that he'd made a point of closing the double doors to the bedroom, which at least served to shut out some of the smell. Out of sight, out of mind, so to speak. Mason had already put the pan on the hob to heat up and added the sausages before turning to look at me.

"So, Nathan, last night – before we went out – you asked when you would be starting work. Well, now that little bit of unpleasantness is over, casually nodding in the direction of the bedroom as if what had happened was no more than someone spilling a little red wine on a white carpet, "I can now tell you what we need you to do. This will be your job and the reason we've taken such a special interest in you! But let's get these fine sausages and eggs inside you first to kickstart that old grey matter! There's quite a lot of information you need to remember, and having a hangover isn't an ideal start."

Chapter 13

Meet Your New Boss

Mason finished his breakfast before me but waited patiently for me to finish before coming to collect my plate, knife, and fork. This was the closest he'd physically been to me since he had uncuffed me, and the thought did cross my mind to kill him there and then. What stopped me was knowing that he knew I could kill him at any instance, and it didn't seem to bother him.

Mason started talking with his back to me as he took the plates over to the sink unit.

"Very soon, your new boss will be arriving, and he'll explain your new job to you in detail," and as if by magic, the doorbell rang.

"Ah, that will be Dale now" and Mason quickly dried his hands and started walking to the entrance hall.

I couldn't quite make out the brief conversation they had at the front door, but I could smell it was a male and he was by himself. Their footsteps approached the kitchen and they entered together. Mason's smile was probably due to the look of surprise on my face.

"Nathan, let me introduce you to Chief of Atlanta Police, Dale Carson."

Chief Carson was in full working uniform and looked about fifty with a grey crew cut. He looked like ex-armed forces, and I could tell that he'd once been in great shape, but perhaps due to being middle-aged, he'd let himself go, and what used to be muscle had largely turned to fat. His face gave absolutely nothing away and it was noticeable he made no effort to come and shake my hand, not that I would have re- ciprocated anyway.

"Hi, Nathan. Are you okay with me calling you Nathan?" He didn't wait for a response but continued speaking while pulling out a seat at the opposite end of the breakfast bar. It was almost like a police interview, no greeting or a shake of the hand, just straight down to business.

"From tomorrow, Nathan, you will be a uniformed sergeant in my force. It will be your first day on the division since your transfer up from Valdosta for a specialist assignment. I'll be back first thing tomorrow to pick you up at 0700. Make sure you are ready in your uniform and don't be late, I won't tolerate any sloppiness."

Carson pushed back his chair to stand up, but I beat him to it. For a brief moment, we just stood there leaning against the table, staring across at each other. I could tell my confrontational stance didn't faze him at all. Perhaps he was ex-military after all, or maybe one of my kind and was very good at covering it up like Lucy was. Or maybe it was because – like Mason – he had something on me that bound my loyalty to him? Well, at least for now, he might, but he didn't need to know that.

"Now, wait a minute, Dale," I began.

"It's 'Mr Carson', 'Sir' or 'Chief' to you", he barked and as if he suddenly realized how menacing he sounded, he forced a half smile and said, "You're in the South now Nathan where everyone is addressed as 'sir' out of common courtesy."

I decided to play along with the game. "I'm sorry, Chief (making a point of not calling him 'sir'), but I have a few questions."

I had more than a few, but only three immediately sprang to

mind.

"You said you dressed in uniform; what uniform? And won't

the other officers think it strange when I just pitch up? And what special assignment?"

It was Mason who answered first.

"I'm surprised you haven't seen your uniform; it's hung up in the other spare bedroom closet. I'm sure it will be a perfect fit because we've done quite a bit of research on you, Mr Cartwright," finishing off with a cross between a smile and a smirk.

It wasn't lost on me that he'd used my title rather than my first name, maybe to impress Carson or to establish his authority, but either way, I wasn't going to let the prick know it bothered me, so I didn't respond.

"The other officers won't be surprised to see you," Carson said in a deadpan tone, "I've already briefed them that you're being drafted in for a specialized assignment, and because it's specialized, they know not to ask questions – it has a 'need to know' classification. Although you are bringing in donuts for your first day, it wouldn't do any harm. Isn't that what you Brits think we do all day, eat Twinkies and donuts all day?"

Enough was enough, and looking directly at Carson, I responded with, "I don't give a shit what you think, fat boy."

That definitely touched a nerve as I saw him immediately stiffen and clench his fists. He was already starting to move around the table to me, but then immediately checked himself, struggled to look more relaxed and even tried and failed to smile.

"I'll give you that one, Cartwright; you're obviously still a bit raw from when you woke up this morning and saw that 'unfortunate' girl." He was just short of doing the bunny ears mime of inverted commas when he said unfortunate, and I wondered if he'd realized that if he had done that, he would have been dead before he'd finished the sentence. I don't think he had any idea, as he was already sitting down and motioning with his hand for me to do the same.

"Okay, let's address the last question you asked Nathan about your assignment."

It wasn't lost on me that he'd reverted to calling me Nathan, it appears you don't need two cops to play 'good cop – bad cop', it can be done by just one control freak with an inferiority complex. I sat down and didn't respond; I needed to fully digest what the still half-blushing chief was about to tell me.

Chapter 14

Your mission, should you choose to accept it

Mason poured a cup of coffee for him and Carson and a third for me, not even asking if I'd prefer tea. To be fair, although breakfast had cured my hangover, the lack of sleep was still hovering in the background, and besides, I needed to listen to what Carson was going to tell me.

Carson took a sip of his black coffee and nodded his approval at Mason before speaking.

"I'll tell you the whole plan and it's quite intensive, so please try and keep questions to a minimum, or at least until the end.

"Unless you've had your head completely in the sand, you must be aware that in two days, the Republican Presidential Nominee, Gerry Miles, will be holding a rally in an open-air stadium in Atlanta. During the event, he will be introducing a visiting dignitary from the UK, one of his main financial donors. Although security will be very tight, you'll be positioned right at the front on crowd control. When the dignitary is brought up on stage, and the two shake hands, you are to shoot the guest.

"Go on then, ask your questions," Carson must have registered my incredulity!

"Well, to start with, why me? I mean, why can't you just do it? Why do you think I'll be better than your people? I mean, I've never even shot a gun!" which, of course, was a lie.

"Oh, come now, sir," responded Carson. "I'm sure you must realize it would be a suicide mission; Senator Miles will have his secret service people all over the place. But you, you see, we know what you are, and we know how fast your type can heal, so you may actually come out of this alive! And besides, you don't really have any choice following last night's little escapade," indicating with his thumb the direction of the bedroom.

"Well, you can go blow yourself," I said with anger in my voice that even surprised me, "I'd rather take my chance with your phony murder wrap than risk dying for a cause that means nothing to me. Find some other mug! I'm out of here, and don't you dare try to stop me, as I'm just looking for the slightest excuse not to rip you two up. And what happened to that poor girl won't be nothing compared to what I'll do to you." I stood up to leave, giving no thought to where I'd go and where my passport and money might be after last night.

I fully expected a fat boy to go for his sidearm, but instead, he reached up to his top pocket and pulled out what appeared to be a photo.

"Perhaps you may wish to reconsider," said Carson, sliding the photo across the table to me. "Apparently you know this young lady."

I turned over the facedown photo and couldn't believe my eyes; it was the lovely Julia. But not the Julia as I remembered her, but a young lady looking terrified with a knife to her throat.

"You see, we kinda expected a response like that, Mr Cartwright, so I guess we made the right decision in taking out a little additional insurance. Of course, I don't need to tell you that if you don't fully cooperate with us, well, I mean, that poor girl, so young and sweet, would be such a damn shame." Carson didn't need to go on; he

99

knew they had me over a barrel.

"We'll go over the finer details tomorrow after I pick you up. I reckon you'll look really fetchin in your uniform, and please don't take this personally! What I *can* tell you is that *should* you come out of this alive, you'll be free to live your life as you please, and I guarantee that the young lady will not be harmed. See you at 0700!"

And with that Carson stood up, whispered something to Mason, placed on his hat faking tipping it to me, and then headed for the front door.

I didn't say anything; I was too busy staring at Julia. The poor thing looked absolutely petrified. Unconsciously, I made the decision there and then that if I did get out of this alive, everyone involved in this charade would be hunted down and killed like a dog. If they wanted a 'vampire,' then they'll bloody well get one!

Perhaps Mason could see I was bubbling under the surface with anger, so he wisely kept to the other side of the table and took a sip of his coffee while never once taking his eyes off me.

"Hey listen", he opened up with, "I realize this isn't an average morning and appreciate you've got a lot to get your head around and I'm guessing you could do that a lot easier without me being here. Tell you what, why don't I drop you off downtown so you can have a coffee and maybe a few adult beverages to help you settle down?"

He reached into the back pocket of his jeans and fished out a mobile phone, which he then slid across the table.

"The address for the house is in the notes on the phone and the Uber service around here is excellent, so come back whenever you want, but please remember the 0700 start tomorrow!"

I looked down at the phone and was about to speak, but

Mason got in there first.

"You seriously didn't think we were going to let you have your own cell, did you? Oh, come on Nathan we're not stupid, and of course, your passport isn't where you left it; however, your money and credit cards are still all there. Tell you what, I'll meet you here in 15 minutes, which will give you time for a quick shower and perhaps put a few more clothes on.

Only then did I remember I was only in my jockey briefs. I got up to do as he suggested, but he interrupted me.

"Probably best to use the shower in the other spare bedroom", indicating the opposite direction to where I was about to head. "I'll grab you some clothes and your money and credit cards."

I was losing my grip. I'd almost forgotten my bedroom was a bloodbath with a dead girl in there – I'd even got used to the smell. I definitely needed that drink downtown.

The shower felt fantastic, starting lovely and hot before I turned it down to a temperature just pleasantly warm. For quite a long time, I just stood there, my mind just swimming with thoughts and emotions, no more so than for Julia. How can a person miss a girl so much when they literally hardly know her? Stepping out of the shower, I found myself staring into a full-length mirror, which hadn't been misted up partly due to me not running the shower hot, but more so, the sheer size of the bathroom. The image that stared back at me caused my first smile of the day – yep, I'd still got it! Although I did not have a particularly muscular physique, basically because I was too lazy to exercise, there was no trace of any fat, and what muscles I had were clearly defined. And in this light, I did actually look more tanned than I thought, which contrasted with my shoulder-length straight blond hair and blue eyes. In essence, I was an averagely good-looking bloke with an average body. This got me thinking that perhaps this was part of a vampire's DNA – designed not to stand out in a crowd or be particularly memorable. However, now was not the time to ponder such trivia as I had more serious issues, the first of which was where my clothes were. I opened the bathroom door, and there they were, neatly folded on the wooden floor just outside the door, with my cash and credit cards on top. As much as I now hated Mason with a passion, I had to give him credit; everything matched and had clearly been folded to a very high standard, certainly not like the pile I would have left them in.

I thanked Mason for the lift as I was opening the car door, making a point not to even look at him. The short journey downtown had been driven in silence with the radio tuned to 93.7 'light rock', which I'm sure had been turned up louder than it needed to be. Perhaps Mason felt a little nervous being in the car alone with me in such close proximity. And so he should, but as they say, 'revenge is a dish best served cold'. The shit had it coming, but not for a while; I needed more information first to ensure Julia's safety.

Georgia's oppressive heat hit me the second I stepped from the car's air conditioning and I was surprised at the number of bars and restaurants there was to choose from in such close proximity. As usual, I didn't select the fanciest looking nor the cheapest looking, but instead opted for one just to my left that was serving lunch and seemed quite popular with the locals. Mediocre is what kept me alive for all those years, and I wasn't going to buck the trend now.

The bar seemed unusually dark inside, but I suppose that was because I'd stepped out of the blaring sunshine. I then realized that I still had my shades on (something you usually didn't have to worry about back in good ol' Blighty!). I quickly removed them, surreptitiously glancing around the bar to see if anyone had noticed my faux pas. Thankfully, most people were either eating, drinking, or engaged in conversation, so I wandered up to the bar and hoisted myself up onto the bar stool.

Pouring through the bar menu, I tried to find a drink that might resemble a half-decent British beer, but as usual, it was all disco piss lager. Instead, I ordered a spiced rum and coke, which, following a look of sheer bemusement, the bartender informed me was called a 'Captains and Coke' over here.

My order caught the attention of the guy who sat to my left, who opened up the conversation by saying, "I guess you're not from around here, friend", the same line I'd got so used to hearing at the bar in Perry last night.

However, it wasn't the redneck in the dirty baseball cap who had my attention. The smell had hit me in seconds! The young black girl sitting to his immediate left was clearly just about to start her period, so I just smiled at the redneck and asked if he minded scooting up to the right as I was partially deaf in my right ear and sitting on his other side would make it easier for me to hear him. He gladly obliged, and no sooner had I sat down did the young girl flash me a huge smile, saying, "Gee, I love your accent; where are you from, Australia?". I gave her my best smile back before explaining that I was actually English, which seemed to make me even more appealing to her. She didn't yet know it, but we were about to become very good friends, and after what I'd been through today, I needed some additional sustenance. This was going to end a better day than it started; I'd played this game for many years.

Chapter 15

An Unexpected Twist

The Uber pulled into the driveway behind Mason's car. Having had a few drinks followed by a visit to the lovely Chantelle's home, or, to be more accurate, 'shack,' for some much-needed revitalizing fluid, I was in no mood to make idle chit-chat with that particular dick head. I had already made my mind up to go straight to bed, a bed which hopefully didn't look like it did this morning.

Entering the unlocked front door, the house seemed very quiet with only the kitchen and hall lights on. I turned right and made my way down to my bedroom. The smell from the morning had certainly gone so reaching for the door handle I was feeling a little more optimistic.

The room was immaculate. Aside from crisp new bedding, it looked no different from when I first arrived, with no hint of blood on the floor (an advantage of having wooden floors, I suppose, and something probably worth remembering) and no trace of the poor girl's corpse.

'Impressive, I think you'll agree."

I jumped so much I nearly shat myself. Turning around to where the voice had come from, I found myself staring open-mouthed in shock at someone I had least expected to see. It shouldn't have come as a surprise, really; I'd only experienced this twice before – someone creeping up on me without me even sensing it – once during the fight with the two yobs a few days ago and then again in my bedsit. And yet here she was again, barely stifling a giggle with her hand over her mouth – Lucy hadn't changed!

"Well, someone's a little jumpy, aren't they? Hello Nathan, it's good to see you again, despite the circumstances."

Lucy didn't wait for a response but instead continued in her usual business-like manner, something I'd got used to.

"Before you go to bed we need to have a little chat, let's go to the kitchen and talk over a cup of tea."

And with that, she gently took my arm and started to walk back to the kitchen while I made a conscious decision to close my mouth, which was still hanging open in shock.

"But what about the owner who lives here?", I asked while sitting down on the seat she had pulled out for me on her way to the kettle. Lucy never ceased to amaze me with her composure; it was as if she'd been living in the house for years!

"Oh, I wouldn't worry about Mr. Green", she said while filling up the kettle, and then turning to look directly at me over her shoulder, "you won't be seeing him again."

I couldn't even remember Mason's surname.

The way she looked at me instantly stopped me from asking any more questions about Mason, and believe me, I had many. I already knew what Lucy was capable of, and just that look she gave me was enough to tell me that particular conversation was, for now, off-limits.

Lucy flicked on the kettle and again, surprisingly, went straight to the cupboard where the cups were kept. Taking two out and adding two tea bags and sweeteners, she turned again to face me, leaning back against the worktop and crossing her arms.

"I've got a lot to tell you, Nathan, but I'll keep it brief as I know you have to be up early tomorrow for your big day."

"Oh, don't worry too much as I think it's just a meet and greet day; you mean I still have to go? And how do you know about it? Where do you fit into all this?"

I was about to go on but was silenced by Lucy putting her finger to her lips and just saying 'Shhh'.

"I appreciate there's an awful lot for me to cover, so if you just let me speak for a while and then at the end you can ask as many questions as you wish." The pop of the kettle switch prompted her to turn around and start pouring the two teas in silence. She brought over the two cups of tea and then again surprised me by sitting down next to me rather than across the table.

"First things first," she said while gently putting her hand over mine, "I imagine you want to know about Julia. The bottom line is we don't yet know where she is, but I assure you we'll find her. I knew she was in trouble yesterday when I texted her to ask what the weather was like over there, and she failed to respond with 'Why, are you planning on visiting.' Instead, I got a 'it's okay', so knew the text wasn't written by her. However, by the time our people got there, both she and the person she was supposed to be looking after had already gone.

"So, about tomorrow. It's not a 'meet and greet' as you so eloquently put it; tomorrow is the day of the assassination, and yes, you are expected to go ahead with it as the chief described."

This question couldn't be held to the end!

"What do you mean 'go ahead'? Are you in on this madness?" I could barely restrain the surprise in my voice. "You really want me to kill someone in public?"

Lucy took a sip of her tea before responding as if choosing her words very carefully.

"Unfortunately, yes, Nathan. You see, the person we need to kill is a genuine threat to world order, and up until this opportunity, we've never been able to get near him because of his security. When your target meets Gerry Miles, he won't have his security detail near him, and with you being right at the front will give you a clear shot at him. You must put at least 3 rounds in him as we can't risk him surviving this; however, no headshots as we need the cameras to clearly show who has been shot. Do you understand?"

"But why me?" I asked genuinely, "I mean, why not someone more experienced, like yourself?" 'Experienced' sounded better than 'older,' 'faster', or 'stronger.'

"Because no one knows who you are over here and you'll blend in. A strikingly good-looking girl dressed in a police uniform at the front of the crowd would, I think, attract attention." I noticed that when she said 'strikingly good-looking,' she gave me a half wink combined with a quick smile, which proved she wasn't serious all the time. And to be fair, looking at her now and imagining her in a police uniform…well, she made a good point!

"And that, Nathan, is all you need to know for the time being; you need to get some rest now for your starring role tomorrow. And don't worry, I promise you'll come out of all this okay", she said again, placing her hand briefly on mine, "you've got a lot of people supporting you."

"I guess you're right; it has been quite a day," I replied, rising from my seat and turning towards my bedroom, "Night, Lucy."

I was halfway down the hallway before Lucy responded.

Already washing the cups, she spoke to me without looking over her shoulder.

"Goodnight, Nathan. Oh, and in the morning, make sure you're outside waiting for the chief before he arrives. I don't want him in here, and it would be better all-around if you don't mention me being here and Mason not being."

It was only then that she looked over at me with a facial expression that told me her last sentence wasn't a 'request'. But almost immediately, she turned on a big beaming smile and said, "Night, love, try and sleep tight, and I'll see you tomorrow night!"

I quietly closed my bedroom door behind me. I'd no idea how I was going to be able to sleep tonight, but Chantelle's earlier donation to the cause certainly had me feeling stronger. It also wasn't lost on me how positive Lucy had been when she said she would see me tomorrow night. I was sure 'Chief Fat-Knacker' would fill me in on the rest of the details.

Anyway, I had no choice; this was for Julia.

Chapter 16

The Dirty Deed

I must admit, the uniform did make me look good, even with the new shorter hair. As soon as I'd put it on, I realized my shoulder-length hair looked so out of place. That was soon fixed with another shower and some kitchen scissors. It probably blocked the shower drain, but I couldn't give a toss; it wasn't likely I would be returning to this house in the near future.

I was still looking at my reflection in the glass-paneled front door when I heard the car pull up at the bottom of the drive. I placed on my mirrored shades and started the quick descent to the car.

Chief Carson wasn't one for pleasantries, ignoring my 'good morning, Chief.' I'd already made up my mind to be extremely courteous and try to get him to open up a bit to me. It didn't matter that I would soon have to kill him; maybe Lucy's persona was rubbing off on me. Instead, Carson went all business-like and, without even looking at me, started to pull away and actually made that tire-screeching noise they all do in the movies as he went around the turning circle at the end of the road.

"First, we'll be going to the Operations Centre in Atlanta to get a briefing and then we'll head to the stadium. When you get the security brief, you'll be LS2,'Local Security 2', you need to remember that. If nothing else, remember the position in the stadium you'll be stationed at. When facing the stage, the guest will walk on from your right. You don't have problems knowing your left from right do you?"

My first impulse was to say, 'They are as different as a salad and a pot of gravy, something you obviously have trouble differentiating between', but thankfully, I regained my senses just in time.

"I'm sure Mason gave you a more than adequate briefing last night," he continued, "so I won't bother repeating it. Just do what he told you to do, and you'll be fine." With that, he turned up the radio and turned onto the slip road for the I-75 to Atlanta.

The rest of the journey was conducted in complete silence and for the next hour I made it look like I was sleeping so he wouldn't interrupt me. However, I must have actually dozed off anyway because the next thing I knew was the speed bump outside the operations centre jolting me awake.

I don't know why, but I'd envisaged a big glass building like New Scotland Yard, but this was like an old inner-city 1970s cinema. The inside belied the impression of its exterior, though, as I followed Carson to a well-lit reception desk manned by a desk sergeant who had obviously seen better days.

"This is Sergeant Nathan Cartwright on special secondment; you should already have a badge made up for him."

The desk jockey didn't even look up at Carson and, more surprisingly, didn't even look at me. I could have been wearing a balaclava and carrying an AK-47, but I don't think he would have noticed. Instead, he was flipping through a box of IDs and, after a few seconds, pulled out a badge on a lanyard. He gave it to Carson, who, in turn, passed it to me.

"Make sure you wear that clearly visible at all times until we get to the stadium later."

Carson then muttered something to the old man which I didn't quite get as I was more fascinated by how the ID card had a

110

recent photo of me, a photo I couldn't even remember being taken. Without any encouragement, Carson then set off at a brisk pace down a long corridor beckoning me to follow. After about 50 feet, he put out his right arm briskly causing me to nearly bump into it.

"Those are the restrooms," he said, "the restrooms are the only place you'll go outside the briefing room," indicating doors directly opposite on the left. "At all times, you'll be with me. You'll sit next to me in the briefing room and say nothing. Even when you go for a piss, I'll be pissing next to you. Do you understand?"

"What about if you need a piss and I don't?" I responded, "I mean, being your age and all that."

It may have been because he was an American and the sarcasm went straight over his head, but the look of pure hatred he gave me suggested ordinarily he would have punched my lights out but had been told not to. Either way, he did get it because he growled "Don't get sassy with me boy". I couldn't help but smile, knowing I was now indispensable for the day. Score one to me!

We were off again, peeling left to enter the conference room. Surprisingly, Carson headed straight to the front row and sat down halfway along the row facing the left of the stage and indicated for me to sit down next to him. It was probably because he was Chief of Police that he was expected to sit on the front row, but it didn't make me comfortable. I'd spent decades being the grey man, and sitting in such a prominent position made my senses heighten. To be fair, no one seemed to notice. The room was perhaps two-thirds full of both uniformed police and some plain-clothed police – or perhaps they were Miles' own security detail, or maybe FBI/CIA?

My thoughts were interrupted by the entrance of 2 plain-clothed males, both dressed in black, walking onto the stage. It appears Men in Black isn't far off the mark after all. I then started to wonder if they all drove around in those big, black, shiny SUVs like all the FBI and CIA do in the movies to make them inconspicuous.

The large screen behind them sprung to life with what appeared to be a huge aerial view of the stadium with markers indicating the speaker's podium, the VIP area, etc., and, more importantly, for us, red markers detailing where all security would be positioned. I quickly found the 'LS2' label showing where I would be standing, right in front of the podium in the gap between the stage and the VIP area at the front. Appreciating the task I was to perform, I looked at what security would be around me and whether I was in their line of fire. I assumed the label 'SD' meant Security Detail, so it would probably be Secret Service plain-clothed security. Most of these were to the back of the staged area to give them a better view of the crowd, which made sense. Fortunately for me, the speaker's podium was situated between me and the 2 SD agents at the back center, so in theory, they shouldn't know what was going on until after the event. My only real concern (apart from the rooftop snipers, of course) was the two Local Security dudes situated on each side of me, perhaps 20 feet away – they would have clear shots at me. Whatever was to happen, I made the decision there and then that as soon as I fired off the 3 shots, I would immediately hit the deck to present a smaller target and get out of sight of the snipers.

I nudged Carson and, keeping my voice as low as possible, asked him why I hadn't been given a bulletproof vest.

"Because people need to see you are getting shot," he whispered back through a positively sinister sneer; "you can't beat a bit of blood for the cameras!" I could tell by the glint in his eye that he couldn't wait for me to get shot and knew he wouldn't give a damn if I didn't pull through. Score one to him.

I was going to ask another question, but the two Men in Black started to talk about radio frequencies and what channels to use. At that point, I just started to go through my own priorities, trying to commit the stadium layout to memory. I wasn't interested in the radio stuff because even if someone called me up, I wasn't going to answer. It would only take someone to use code, like 'What's your 7?' and I would be screwed.

They then started to brief us all on the itinerary. Gerry Miles would start by thanking all his government cronies in attendance who would be sitting in the VIP enclosure in front of me. He would then go into his speech, and at some point, he would introduce his guest benefactor to the stage. The benefactor would come from the stage left alone and shake hands with Miles. Hopefully, Miles would step out from behind the podium to meet his guest. Otherwise, my line of sight could be cut off when they shook hands. This would mean me having to move to the side to get a better view of them both, and any movement, as seen in nature, usually attracts unwanted attention. My head must have been all over the place, consciously playing through all the possible scenarios because the end of the briefing completely took me by surprise.

Carson was one of the first to stand, looking down at me with a faceless expression.

"Come on, Cartwright, it's time to leave. Let's get to the food hall before the rest of this mob. Give you a chance to get some donuts down. You know you're officially a cop." I was sure this was his weak attempt at humor, but even if it was funny, the fact that he'd addressed me by my last name prevented me from rising to the bait. Sometimes staying silent following an act of provocation, however mild, makes you look the stronger man, so without any acknowledgment, I rose up and gestured to him to take the lead, which he did. I just followed on, feeling like a bloody lap dog following his master. Again, the only motivation that stopped me just walking out the door was Julia, I had to follow this charade through no matter what.

It shouldn't have surprised me, but it did. For a good part of the morning, I'd spent most of my time staring at an overhead graphic of the stadium and looking at the labels, denoting where everyone would be. I suppose your brain unconsciously looks at the size of the labels and scales the stadium to suit, so walking into the stadium, I was initially stunned by the size. While taking in the roof line, my attention was drawn to movement on the east side of the roof. It was one of the snipers pre-positioning him/herself, thankfully, where I remembered they should be.

"I've got to go and talk to some people", Carson exclaimed, interrupting my train of thought. "Have a walk around just to get your bearings and get to know where you'll be stationed. Focus on what you're here to do; the VIP benefactor must die today, so make sure of it. Keep your head clear and wait for that ideal opportunity. Oh, and while I remember, make sure now the safety is off on your revolver. You will have very little time as it is, and the last thing I want to see is you pull your gun, aim it, and then you are just standing there trying to pull a trigger that won't move! In fact, give it here." Without asking, he unclipped the strap, securing my revolver in its holster, took it out, and flicked off the safety catch before replacing it in the holster but leaving the strap off.

"I guess that must really hurt, having a loaded weapon with the safety off next to someone you clearly hate, eh boy?" Carson was clearly enjoying his little power trip.

"Why don't you just jog on a fat boy before the other members of the Village People start wondering where you are? Best you waddle along now then, fat man."

That clearly hit the mark as he actually took a step towards me with pure hate all over his face before stopping himself and forcing a fake smile. Carson then tipped his hat to me.

"Y'all have a nice day now, and I'm sure you will!" and Carson rolled on his heels, turning away from me sniggering to himself.

I don't think he understood that a nice day for me would be the day I met up with him and his buddy Mason again, assuming I survived that day. Oh yeah, that would be one hell of a nice day alright.

After mulling around trying to look like I knew what I was doing I started glancing around trying to find a place to sit in the shade. The sun was already scorching hot, and the black uniform didn't help one bit. At that point, a gentleman in a suit approached me pulling a wheeled container. As he got to me, he stopped and reached down to open the container and produced three bottles of what felt like ice-cold water.

"Make sure you stay hydrated, officer," and then started to walk off, not waiting for an answer. This was probably a good thing because my attempt at saying thanks in my best American accent was truly appalling, to the extent that it nearly made me laugh. The smile that caused me made me realize how parched my lips already were. I'd finished the first bottle before I even reached my seat in the shade, which caused an ice cream headache that made me wince.

Two hours later the stadium was three-quarters full. Music was already blaring out of the speakers, trying to keep the crowd entertained. The crowd were certainly better dressed for the weather than I was, with most of them wearing hats and then either a t-shirt or vest.

Finally, after a few warm-up speeches from people I'd never seen before from the VIP area, the main attraction made his way onto the stage. The crowd went mad, cheering like they were witnessing the second coming. After soaking up the applause and chanting for what seemed like forever, the Republican Presidential Candidate Gerry Miles finally started his speech. Well, I say speech, but it quickly degenerated into him just slagging people off but the rednecks were lapping it up. I remember listening to the radio during the 1940s to Churchill's speeches, in which he galvanized the country, bringing everyone together to fight for a single and just cause. Yet this bloke seemed to be taking the piss out of everyone who wasn't cheering him on in the stadium. This was certainly one screwed-up country when it came to politics, and I thought the UK was bad! This 'ranting' for want of a better expression continued for about an hour or so before it seemed he was running out of ideas. At this point, he gestured to his left and shouted at the crowd.

"We have a very special guest here today that I'd like to introduce to you! One of the Party's biggest financial benefactors and someone who really knows what we can do for this country and why we're going to win it."

This was my moment. I turned to face the right side of the stage, keeping my hand touching the butt of my sidearm, ready to spring into action.

"All the way from England, I give you, Lord Peterson!"

The crowd erupted while I just froze in disbelief! Why had no one told me the target was my dad? I mean, in hindsight, it was bloody obvious why they didn't, and now a situation was playing out in slow motion, and I didn't know what to do. My dad was now only a few feet from Miles, and literally, in the second or so before he went to grasp the candidate's hand, he did something extraordinary. My dad glanced directly at me, gave a brief nod of the head, and winked at me. He knew! He knew I'd be there standing exactly where I was, and he was in on the whole thing! I don't know why, but that was all I needed to see.

My three fingers of my right hand closed around the butt of the gun, and within a flash, it was out of the holster and pointing at my dad. Because everyone in the VIP area was looking up at the stage, no one seemed to notice me until that first squeeze of the trigger, and even then, I'd gotten off all three shots before the screaming and panicking started. I immediately dropped the gun and almost instantaneously was flung around, followed by a huge punch to the back, causing me to twist around and fall on my back. While falling, I could see the puffs of dust all around me as the shots came in, but by the time I hit the ground, I was unconscious, with everything having gone quiet and black.

Chapter 17

Revelations

I tried to open my eyes, but regardless of my efforts, they felt like they were glued shut. I felt cold water being gently applied, and my right eye slowly started to open before the same attention was applied to my left eye. That, too, slowly started to unstick itself. The light was blinding, but within a few seconds and after much blinking, I was able to focus on what seemed to be a plain white ceiling with embedded fluorescent lights, the type you get in a hospital. I tried to sit up, using my arms to prop myself up, but the searing jolt of pain in my left shoulder caused me to drop back down again.

A female voice broke through the silence.

"Marie, you can bring our guests through now, seeing as our hero is finally waking up."

I recognized that voice and turned my head to the right to focus on who was speaking. It was Lucy, of course, although she looked far more businesslike than usual due to her hair being pinned up in a messy bun. The look suited her. The more I got to know this lady, the better she looked—an understated natural beauty.

I broke into a smile for some reason, expecting another jolt of pain, which never came.

"I'm in hospital? But I thought we didn't use hospitals because of the tests…"

I was cut off by Lucy, who was pointing somewhere to my left, above and behind my head.

"Yes, that alone would freak them out. Your resting pulse is slightly high because, obviously, you're recovering, but if a normal hospital saw that pulse of 34, they'd probably have the defibrillator out by now, and you really would be dead!"

I turned to look where she was pointing and for the first time saw the monitors. I hadn't noticed them because, unlike the movies when they always do that beeping, it actually must be very annoying and I'd been told that most hospitals keep them on silent.

"Our extremely low pulse is one of the reasons our people can move so fast. Imagine if you moved as fast as you can with a normal pulse of 80, you'd have a heart attack within seconds!"

Lucy took my right hand in hers and continued, "From what I was told, the low pulse rate developed over many millennia when our people used to have to sleep through the days and only come out at night to hunt for fear of being caught. Sleeping through the day is always difficult, so thankfully, we've moved on since then, but the pulse is a legacy of those times."

Lucy was interrupted by the door opening behind her, and she immediately let go of my hand. In walked two smartly dressed gentlemen, the first of whom needed no introduction.

"I'm so sorry, Dad," I said while at the same time wondering why he looked no different from when he'd walked on that stage. I mean, I'd put at least 3 rounds in him!

My father just laughed!

"I can see the confusion on your face, Nathan, you never were good at hiding your emotions! Thank you, but I'm actually fine, I was wearing a bulletproof vest because I knew you'd step up to the mark when asked to. I imagine you've got lots of questions unless Lucy's already back briefed you already" and he glanced at Lucy.

"I haven't, Sir; I thought it would be better coming from you."

The use of 'Sir' and the slight bowing of her head when speaking to my dad didn't go unnoticed by me.

My father pulled up a leather reclining chair, which I imagined wasn't standard inventory in normal hospitals. This was a heavy piece of kit, but he moved it effortlessly with one hand, not dragging it but lifting it clear of the floor as if it were a plastic garden chair.

"You don't mind, do you?" he said, indicating to the chair, but the question was rhetorical since he'd already sat down, crossing his leg to reveal obviously expensive shoes to match his equally expensive tailored suit. He turned his gaze on me and began speaking in a very cultured and eloquent tone, befitting a Peer of the Realm.

"You see, what you did, Nathan, was only part of the bigger mission; you were there only as a means of distraction. The mission objective was to eliminate Gerry Miles, and that dear boy was a resounding success! You see, getting close to that obnoxious individual is nigh impossible due to his security detail and paranoia. Granted, it cost me an extortionate amount of money in backing his campaign to finally get an invitation to get that close to him, but the last thing America, and indeed the free world, needed was a narcissistic despot determined to become a real-life Bond villain as their President and Commander in Chief. It doesn't bear thinking about, and believe me, boy, having lived through every war since the Crusades, I've seen some crazy dictators in my time, and this idiot was right up there with the worst!"

"But how?" I asked, "I'm sure I only shot you. I'm sorry when I said 'only...'",

I could actually feel myself reddening with a mixture of shame and embarrassment.

My dad threw is head back and the booming laugh that came out filled the room, even to the extent that the man who he came in with him turned around from the coffee machine he was helping himself to and smiled.

"It wasn't you who killed him, Nathan. It was me! You see, after your third shot, I knew everyone would be focused on either you or the idiot next to me; no one would care about a British Lord getting shot. And, of course, the natural reflex defensive position is to cross your arms in front of your face. This gave me the ideal opportunity to pull a snub-nosed revolver out of my sleeve and put a round through his face before returning it to my sleeve. I used one of those hollow point rounds, you know, took the back of his head clean off, so it did. Of course, they are illegal in the UK, but over here, well, it's America, isn't it?" he said, smiling sarcastically. "Used to call them 'dum-dum' bullets during the war, you know." I could briefly see his mind drifting off, remembering days gone by. I wondered what it must be like to have so many memories, but then focused back to the matters at hand.

"But surely, with the press and TV coverage and the super frame-by-frame slow motion they have now, someone will have a picture of you firing the gun?"

"Ah, but the crossing of the arms would have shielded the gun from most of the shots you see," and the theatrical way my dad was replaying the event with his arms flying while speaking seemed almost comical.

Lucy interrupted unexpectedly.

"I know you're still skeptical, Nathan, and many years ago, I was the same. But what your father isn't telling you is the speed it happened. You see, he's quite capable of pulling that gun, firing it off, and returning it to his sleeve faster than any camera frame speed. It comes with age and maturity. Hopefully, one day you'll grow up to match his strength and speed."

My dad was looking at Lucy with a look of fondness I hadn't seen before. He obviously trusted her completely and I was so glad she was on our side.

My mind was still buzzing.

"But what about Chief Carson and Julia? What's happened to Julia, and why is she involved in this? Is she okay?" I looked directly at Lucy, but it was my dad who spoke first.

"Settle down, my boy; it will all become clear in a minute; you have nothing to worry about! But I'll let Lucy take over for a while, and you don't want to hear it from a bumbling old fool!"

There was no way that man was a fool, despite being extremely old, but Lucy took on the story anyway.

"Firstly, Julia is fine, I promise you!" she said sitting back in her chair as if in it for the long haul.

"When Mason decided to leave us at the house, let's just say he didn't go too willingly, and when being questioned by our people, it turned out he started to feel a little uncomfortable with the whole process and told us exactly where to find her. He won't be bothering you again." She said the last sentence, looking directly into my eyes, leaving me in no doubt that Mason had met some sort of grizzly end. Good, the prick deserved it and saved me a job!

After a very brief pause to let the information sink in, she continued.

"It also transpired that the person Julia was assigned to look after had been following your little escapade in Halifax via the local press. Unfortunately, although one of our kind, he'd somehow formed an alliance with Mason and Carson, and this alliance stretched right up to the now-dead presidential candidate. You see, they genuinely wanted you to assassinate your father. As you know, your father deals a lot with stocks and shares, and Miles has, sorry, 'had,' an enormous amount of money invested through your dad. But what he couldn't handle was the fact that your father had 'control' over all this wealth, and as you've probably guessed after listening to the candidate's speech yesterday, he is a control freak. He wanted someone under his control to manage the Western world's wealth.

"I suppose I should also mention what happened with Carson because he was the obvious loose end. Well, as it happens, they found him late last night at his home, and it appears he'd put a bullet through his brain with his own revolver. Perhaps understandably, since his only job was keeping the speaker safe, and he ended up with 'three' deaths on his hands." Lucy had done the little bunny ears with her hands when she mentioned the word 'three,' which got me thinking.

I let the Carson 'supposed' cause of death go. I knew it was our people's work. Although Carson was a fat blustering piece of shit, always trying to come across as a hard man with authority, I knew that if the chips were down, he'd be too chicken shit to kill himself.

But how are we?" gesturing to my dad, "here? Surely, I should be banged up in jail or at least a secure hospital?" I'd already forgotten about Lucy's 'three dead' remark.

"My father nodded his head to the right and said, "I'll let the US Secretary for Homeland Security explain that."

Up to this point I'd paid little to no attention to the chap who had entered with my dad. I just assumed he must be his driver, assistant or something. This got him my full attention!

The man walked over from the coffee machine and handed my dad a cup before moving his own cup of coffee to his left hand, holding out his right hand to me. I noticed he hadn't made a cup for Lucy or even asked her if she wanted one, perhaps this is how the old-world order worked.

"Hello Nathan" he said shaking my hand, "I'm Curt, although you may remember me as Michael: you've come a long way since those days at the fayre helping us pack the tents!"

Oh my God, I hadn't even recognized him! He did look older than I remembered. When I knew him, he looked in his twenties, but here was a very debonaire-looking middle-aged man with grey hair. His accent was also a cut-glass English accent, very similar to my Dad's, which made me wonder how he passed off as an American.

"You're probably wondering about my accent", he asked as if he could read my mind, "well I can assure you dear boy that this isn't how I usually speak. Believe it or not, and even if I say so myself, my Virginian accent is more than passable." I saw my dad give an imperceptible nod over Michael's shoulder.

"I'm sure you've got a plethora of questions, so let me try and explain to you what happened today and what will happen over the next few days."

"Thanks for using the word 'plethora', it means a lot to me", I said in a jovial manner.

My dad issued a snort of laughter, throwing his head back, but the joke seemed lost on Michael, who continued in a businesslike manner.

"You see, and as Miss Lucy alluded to earlier", nodding his

appreciation at Lucy, "we've known about this plot for a few days now. However, my official position within the US government allows me to make decisions that no one will ever question.

"One of those decisions was to conduct individual briefings to the security details nearest to you in the stadium – Chief Carson's people, that is, not Miles' security detail of whom I have little control – to shoot near you rather than at you. Of course, they will be all receiving nice bonuses for their families at Christmas. I mean, you must have seen American movies. Once someone has the balls to release the first shot, everyone wants to be the hero, and they all open up; sadly, this is a reflection of our trigger-happy cousins. And that's why you were only hit by two rounds, which, although unfortunate, is actually not a bad result. No offense meant, of course!

"Thankfully, the round that hit your shoulder causing you to spin round, meant the high-velocity round from one of the snipers didn't meet your body perpendicular to the shot but rather caused the round to hit and deflect. Believe me, if that had exited your body, we'd still be scraping parts of you up.

"Then, of course, we had to get you out of there! Fortunately, we had three ambulances at the ready", and with that, he gave me a small wink. "All three casualties were whisked away with a police escort to the local hospital, but to throw off the press, you were both transferred to different ambulances and again left the hospital at staggered times to bring you here. Except for Miles, of course, he was left there for the press and public to feed on."

I remembered my earlier question.

"But Miss Lucy said there were *three* deaths. I decided to use Lucy's formal address to toe the line; if Michael had used it, then it followed, so should I. If nothing else, it demonstrated my respect for authority.

125

My dad interjected. "Actually, Nathan, I was to survive, but unfortunately, not the same for you; officially, you're dead. Thanks to the Secretary for Homeland Security here, a press statement was released saying both you and Gerry Miles had been declared dead on arrival at the hospital."

"But surely, over time, someone will figure out it wasn't me who killed Miles but you."

Michael gave a little huff accompanied by a smile.

"As they like to say over here, this isn't our first rodeo; we've had to play out this diversionary scenario before. You'll obviously remember the JFK assassination and Lee Harvey Oswald's part in it. Well, Lee was actually one of us. Although we told him to try and kill the President – because the president had actually found out about the likes of us and was about to persecute us in public - that old Italian rifle Oswald insisted on using, plus his, let's say 'lack of intelligence' meant that we had to execute the kill ourselves. What we didn't expect was Oswald to start shooting after the president's motorcade had already turned the corner and was heading away from him; I mean, why not shoot when they were approaching the book repository and slowing right down to take the corner? Anyway, that put us in a bit of a pickle, meaning we had to shoot from the opposite direction, which has always added a degree of intrigue within the public domain. Anyhow, I digress. Oswald was supposed to disappear, but again, he didn't follow the plan and got himself caught. This then presented another dilemma: Oswald would never last in jail under questioning, so we had to enlist the help of our associate Jack Ruby."

This completely knocked me out! My dad was behind the JFK assassination! But I needed to get back to matters of the moment. However, I didn't need to say anything, as the mere gesture of my dad casually holding up his hand had caused Michael to stop.

"I'm sorry, Master, I let myself get a little carried away there," said Michael, nodding at my dad.

Michael then returned his attention back to me and continued, unperturbed by my dad asking him to stop with his JFK anecdote.

"You're probably wondering as to what happens from hereon in Nathan. Well, firstly, your father will be transferred to the airport by ambulance tomorrow, where he will be transferred by gurney onto his private jet, just to keep up the pretense of serious injury, you understand. As for you young man, today, as I speak, your lovely Julia is looking around a beautiful little cottage in a town just outside of Edinburgh. Our sources have already told us she is already discussing how she wants it decorated, so it appears that it more than meets her requirements and expectations. She's also more than looking forward to getting back together with you if that's okay with you, of course."

I didn't need to speak as I'm sure my beaming smile must have lit up the room!

"But I'll let Miss Lucy go over the travel details with you. When things have settled down a little, your father said he'd like to visit you in Scotland as he's never had the pleasure of meeting your young lady."

Although he tried to hide it, I could read in my father's eyes that this was indeed true and had nothing to do with 'business.' He blinked a few times before addressing me himself.

"So that's it in a nutshell, my boy. I know it's an awful lot to take in, especially when you didn't sign up for any of this, but you can always ask more questions later. Right now, I'm sure you're a little tired, plus both Michael and I have a few loose ends we need to tie up before departing tomorrow. So, we'll be off now, and Lucy can fill you in on the travel details." And without any of the effort you would expect from an old man, he rose from the chair like an invisible winch was being used and approached my side. He took my hand in a very firm grip and said, "We're all so proud of you, Nathan, and we'll no doubt see you soon."

Without waiting for a response, he turned and headed for the door pursued by Michael who turned and gave me a nod, my dad never looked back.

"Are you okay?" asked Lucy, "I imagine your head's all over the place. I also need to leave but will meet you here first thing tomorrow morning. Is there anything you're not sure about before I leave?"

I did have one final question.

"I know my dad is going to be traveling to the airport in an ambulance, but it was never mentioned about me flying back with him on his jet."

"You and I will be flying back commercially, Nathan. We've already booked the flights for tomorrow."

"But surely someone will recognize me, and the paparazzi will be all over us?"

Lucy pulled out her mobile phone, pressed a few buttons, and handed it to me.

"I very much doubt it", she said.

"Bloody hell!" I exclaimed and then immediately apologized to Lucy for my outburst of language.

Lucy smiled!

"Completely expected" she laughed, it's not every day you go to sleep looking like a seventeen-year-old and wake up in your early thirties!

" It's a good look, you look very handsome and I'm sure Julia will be very appreciative of the new look. Hell, if it wasn't for Julia, I might even fancy you", causing her to laugh again.

"I'll see you about 0700 tomorrow. Get some sleep – you're recovering remarkably well. Any discomfort, please press the bell here, and Maria will attend to your needs. Don't be shy with her; she's married to one of us, as are all our nurses, and being on a salary five times that of a usual nurse, she knows the value of being discreet! I'll also need that back if that's okay with you?" she said while reaching for the phone.

I'd been so preoccupied with my new look that I'm not sure I heard much of what Lucy had just told me. But by now, I'd got used to my new look, and even if I say so myself, it was a bloody good look that I'm sure Julia would love!

Chapter 18

A New Day, a New Dawn

It had been ten months since the assassination, and Scotland had been very kind to Julia and me. Apart from the constant horizontal rain and occasionally freezing temperatures, the people were very friendly, and I loved my new job.

Somehow, and the irony hadn't been lost on me, my dad had managed to secure me a job within the Balmoral royal household maintaining their official and unofficial horse-drawn carriages – Cartwright by name and profession! I suppose when your CV, or resume as the Americans insist on calling it, leads with 'The Honourable' Nathan Cartwright, the job is already practically in the bag!

My bond with my dad had certainly strengthened over this last ten months. Perhaps because of what had happened in America, which, thanks to Michael's work behind the scenes, had now completely blown over, but more so, I think, due to him genuinely bonding with his own flesh and blood. We were now quite close, although written or email conversations between us were still firmly off-limits. Instead, he had given both Julia and me a mobile phone, which we were instructed to use only to contact him. However, when not busy, he would often fly up to spend the odd weekend with us both. Although the little house we had was obviously not up to his usual standard of accommodation, he never complained and had even started to develop a sense of humor! None more so than when he took the piss out of my Yorkshire accent.

"It's my father," he'd tell me, "not 'me dad,'" "while grimacing. "I sometimes wonder why we sent you to that godforsaken land, but I supposed it served its purpose." And then he would laugh like he'd just realized he'd made a joke!

He also loved Julia like his own daughter, the daughter he'd never had. Well, I assumed that was the case, I certainly wasn't going to ask! I had wondered how he'd been on this planet so many years and only had one surviving son, but there are some questions that are sacrosanct; if he wanted to tell us later, that was up to him.

It still made me smile inwardly whenever I thought of Julia. She had instantly bonded with Dad, perhaps for getting her out of that hellhole she'd found herself in being held hostage. She was the only person allowed, or should I say brave enough, to actually take the piss out of my dad, and he seemed to lap it up! He laughed with Julia more than anyone else, including me, which often made me think they were sometimes laughing at me, but it made me so happy.

Oh, and I shouldn't forget Lucy! I remember when Lucy had visited us in the bedsit in Halifax and my first impulse was to kill her, until I realized her power of course, and yet here we were only a few months later and she was genuinely our best friend. She had chilled so much, and gone were the days when she used to follow me around anonymously.

Instead, Lucy quite often took Julia out shopping. Well, I say 'shopping,' but quite often the shopping involved a lunch and a bottle of Pino Grigio between them. They were now inseparable, although Lucy would quite often disappear for weeks at a time on business. What that 'business' entailed, we never asked, that was an unwritten rule everyone understood.

My thoughts were interrupted by the door opening to my right, and Nurse Catherine appeared with a big beaming smile.

"My Lord, Ma'am, Sir, you are now permitted your audience with the Princess, although please remember she is still very tired", and holding the door open with her hand, Catherine gestured us to enter, while I noticed also bowing her head.

Ordinarily, my dad would always enter a room first out of respect, but on this occasion, he motioned me ahead of him.

"Go ahead, Nathan; after all, it's all your own work."

We all entered the room with Lucy bringing up the rear. Julia had propped herself up with her pillows and was nearly sitting upright in bed. I could now see what the delay had been. Catherine had given her a full makeover, she looked absolutely stunning. She needn't have bothered of course, but I'd learned some time ago never to judge a female's logic, if it made them happy, leave it alone.

"Hi everyone", she exclaimed with a beaming smile, do come in and make yourself comfortable, nodding towards the three expensive chairs arranged to one side of the bed.

I looked towards my dad, who nodded at me to take the chair closest to the head of the bed, closest to Juila.

"You both look absolutely wonderful my dear", said my dad before I'd even had the chance to kiss Julia, and that was immediately followed by an "Aw, bless him, he's beautiful!" from Lucy.

They were, of course, referring to our newborn baby boy being cradled gently in Julia's arms.

"Have you thought of a name yet", asked my dad in his usual direct, no-nonsense manner, "as we can't keep referring to him as 'the boy'?", and then he gave the faintest of smiles.

Julia looked at me as if waiting for me to answer, but I said, "You go ahead, after all, you've done all the hard work."

Julia smiled and then addressed my dad and Julia said, "Well obviously Nate for his first name, but he will also have two middle names named after our two favourite people. Meet Nathan Gerald Lucian Cartwright!"

And as if on cue, Baby Nate immediately started to cry and it was like he didn't want to stop. This in turn caused an instant change in Julia's persona with that beaming smile leading to a flood of tears.

"He's probably just hungry", said Lucy trying to give Julia a reassuring smile, "do you want us to pop out for a moment?"

This finally opened the floodgates, and tears started pouring down Julia's face.

"I'm so sorry Nathan", she said looking at me, "but that's the thing, he won't take any food, yet I know he's hungry. Catherine said to wait for you, but I'm scared, he needs to feed!".

I looked at Nurse Catherine for some sort of explanation but saw she and my dad were looking at each other in some sort of silent communication, which culminated in Catherine nodding to my dad.

My dad turned to face Julia.

"Don't worry my princess, we've seen this happen before, it's nothing to worry about. Now if you'll allow me, I just want to try something", he said rising effortlessly from his chair and gliding to the head of the bed as if on invisible roller skates.

Julia looked at me, her tears now subsiding somewhat, and I just nodded to her although totally unaware of what my dad was suggesting. Julia turned to my dad and gave her best-broken smile.

Nurse Catherine had meanwhile approached the side of my dad and handed him a scalpel. This caused Julia's eyes to immediately widen in shock.

My dad saw her change of expression and immediately reassured her, "Don't worry, my dear, I wouldn't dream of hurting someone so precious."

And with that, he made a slight incision in the tip of his left forefinger and before anyone had time to object offered it to the crying baby Nate. The speed at which the baby latched onto my dad's finger surprised everyone and the crying immediately stopped.

My dad then removed his finger after a few seconds, and again, to everyone's surprise, the baby didn't start crying again as expected.

My dad focused firmly on Julia's face, ignoring the rest of us.

"It's as I thought, Julia. Young Nate here is one of our kind. I think you'll find he has no problem taking milk from you now; he just needed a very small aperitif to whet his appetite, something I'm afraid you'll have to get used to. But don't worry, he only needs a tiny amount before feeding. We're not asking you to slaughter a newborn lamb before every meal."

My dad didn't attempt to laugh at his own joke but instead waited to allow this information to sink in with Julia and me.

"But I've no idea how to take care of one of your kind", exclaimed Julia, and looking at me, continued, "There's no way I'm going to give him up to join a bloody fayre like Nathan was!"

She clearly had more to say but my dad ever so gently rested his hand on her shoulder before speaking.

"You won't have to do that, my dear. Things have changed a lot since then, particularly with the ease of movement around the world these days. No, unlike the relationship between Nathan and me, the two of you will be parents to Baby Nate for all of your lives. We will of course have to keep moving you around at certain times for obvious reasons, but we'll look after that aspect.

"This will obviously be harder for you, Julia, as you'll see this beautiful little boy eventually get older than you but never seem to age, but consider this as some form of compensation. How many parents have the chance to give birth to a son knowing that for the whole of his exceedingly long life, he will have people from afar watching and caring over him for his every need? I promise you with all my heart everyone in this room, and some people he may never meet will love and care for this little boy like he was their own.

"Now, I think one certain individual may be rather hungry, so I think it's time to take our leave. I'll see you soon, my dear." And with that, my dad leaned forward to give Julia her usual peck on the cheek. But this time, it was different. Julia latched onto his neck with her free left arm and returned his kiss with real emotion.

"Thank you, Dad, I love you so much", and after a few seconds realized she was still hugging him in a bizarre headlock and let him go.

My dad turned around to face us and for the first time I'd ever seen, he had some colour to his cheeks. Lord Peterson, perhaps the oldest person on the planet who had lived through such scandalous times as the Renaissance Period, the roaring twenties, and the swinging sixties, was actually blushing! And I think he knew that I'd seen it because on his way past me to exit the room, he betrayed his usual deadpan look to issue the briefest embarrassed smile, which disappeared as fast as it had arrived. And that was it; he left the room without even a word as if he was leaving the office after a hard day's work.

Perhaps one day I would turn out like my dad, and maybe that might not be the worst thing that could happen, but at least for the next fifty or so years, I would have the love of a good woman to keep me on the straight and narrow.

www.ingramcontent.com/pod-product-compliance
Ingram Content Group UK Ltd.
Pitfield, Milton Keynes, MK11 3LW, UK
UKHW021805280125
4322UKWH00071B/597